Credit control

Tutorial

Michael Fardon

Published by Osborne Books Limited
Unit 1B Everoak Estate
Bromyard Road, Worcester WR2 5HP
Tel 01905 748071
Email books@osbornebooks.co.uk
Website www.osbornebooks.co.uk

Design by Laura Ingham

Printed by CPI Group (UK) Limited, Croydon, CR0 4YY, on environmentally friendly, acid-free paper from managed forests.

British Library Cataloguing in Publication Data
A catalogue record for this book is available from the British Library

ISBN 978 1909173 408

Contents

Acknowledgements

The publisher wishes to thank Cathy Turner for her help with the reading and production of the book. Thanks are also due to Aubrey Penning for his technical editing and to Laura Ingham for her designs for this new series.

The publisher is indebted to the Association of Accounting Technicians for its help and advice to our authors and editors during the preparation of this text.

Author

Michael Fardon has extensive teaching experience of a wide range of banking, business and accountancy courses at Worcester College of Technology. He now specialises in writing business and financial texts and is General Editor at Osborne Books. He is also an educational consultant and has worked extensively in the areas of vocational business curriculum development.

Introduction

what this book covers

This book has been written specifically to cover the 'Credit control' Unit which is an optional Unit for the revised (2013) AAT Level 4 Diploma in Accounting.

The book contains a clear text with worked examples and case studies, chapter summaries and key terms to help with revision. Each chapter has a wide range of activities, many in the style of the computer-based assessments used by AAT.

Osborne Workbooks

Osborne Workbooks contain practice material which helps students achieve success in their assessments. *Credit Control Workbook* contains a number of paper-based 'fill in' and free text practice exams in the style of the computer-based assessment. Please visit www.osbornebooks.co.uk for further details and access to our online shop.

1 Introduction to credit control

this chapter covers...

Credit control is the process of managing customers who pay on credit so that settlement of debt is made on time.

Efficient credit control is essential for maintaining the liquidity of an organisation; money not received may mean that money will have to be borrowed.

This chapter starts with an overview of the whole credit control process – from credit application to debt collection.

The chapter then concentrates on the ways in which an organisation obtains information which enables them to assess the suitability of:

- *customers who are applying to trade on credit terms*
- *existing customers who have already been granted credit terms*

This assessment process involves:

- *examining the external sources of information – for example, banks, credit rating agencies and other suppliers*
- *examining the internal sources of information available to help with the assessment decision – reports from colleagues (eg sales records, notes on visits) and analysis of financial accounts*

The next chapter describes in detail how a customer is assessed by means of credit analysis of financial accounts made available to the supplier. This will involve the calculation of performance ratios and the application of a credit scoring system.

LIQUIDITY AND CREDIT CONTROL

the importance of liquidity

Liquidity is a measure of the extent to which a person or organisation has cash – or can raise cash – to meet immediate and short-term liabilities.

As you will know from your studies of cash management, **liquidity management** in an organisation involves the **timing** of cash inflows and outflows – including financing and investing – so that the organisation has sufficient working capital and remains solvent.

The main sources of liquidity are – in order of liquidity – cash, bank deposits, trade receivables, and inventory. This book concentrates on the management of **trade receivables** through efficient credit control – the granting of credit, the monitoring of customer accounts and effective collection of debts.

Of course, the need for liquidity management will vary according to the nature of the organisation. For example, businesses such as shops, operate on the basis of **cash sales** and do not run the same **risks** as the business that relies to a greater extent on **credit sales** – ie buy now and pay later.

external methods of improving liquidity

You should note that there are a number of financial services available to organisations which can help them with debt collection and the avoidance of irrecoverable debts. These services are provided by banks, insurance and other financial institutions. They will improve or safeguard the liquidity of the organisation, but at a cost.

These services include:

- **credit insurance** – insuring against the risk of non-payment, both in the UK and overseas – accounts covered can be single customer accounts, key accounts, or general coverage

- **factoring** – a factoring company lends money to a business against the value of its trade receivables. The customer then settles the debt with the factoring company which takes over and runs the sales ledger. This provides the business with liquidity before the invoice due dates

- **invoice discounting** – a finance company lends money against invoices issued to selected customers of the business, but the business continues to operate its own sales ledger and credit management system so that the customer does not realise that the finance company is involved

There is more information about these schemes in Chapter 5, pages 93-94.

THE CREDIT CONTROL FUNCTION – AN OVERVIEW

Credit control is the process of managing customers who pay on credit so that settlement of debt is made on time.

An important element of liquidity management is the efficient functioning of the sales ledger – or in basic terms, customers paying up on time. If customers do not pay up on time, or – worse still – become insolvent, this can be the result of:

■ credit terms being granted to customers who are not creditworthy (a failure in the system when the customer applied for credit), or

■ the payments of the customer not being monitored effectively and warning signs of customer financial problems not being picked up (a failure of the sales ledger management system)

The result in either case will be an irrecoverable debt and loss of profit.

Credit control forms part of the accounting and finance function of an organisation. The number of people employed in credit control will depend on the size of the organisation. It may be a whole department, a section, or in the case of a small business, the accounts assistant or even the proprietor. The credit control activities carried out are summarised in the diagram on the next page, which you should study carefully. They include:

■ assessing new applications for credit (either from new customers or from existing customers looking for an increased credit limit)

■ monitoring sales ledger accounts by using reports such as the receivables (aged trade receivables) summary

■ chasing overdue debts and dealing with irrecoverable debts

Larger organisations are likely to have a **credit control policy**, a written set of procedures detailing issues such as assessment methods, credit terms granted, chasing of debts, and dealing with irrecoverable debts. An example is shown on page 13. It will normally be accompanied by documentation such as credit application forms, sales contracts and chaser letters.

People who work in credit control need to be highly experienced in communication skills: they are negotiators and persuaders, but should also be able to take on the role of rottweilers.

the credit control process

The diagram on the opposite page illustrates all the stages involved in the credit control process. This chapter concentrates on the external and internal sources of information that can be used to reach a decision on whether or not to grant credit terms to a customer. This area of study forms the top part of the diagram, shown inside the dotted line box.

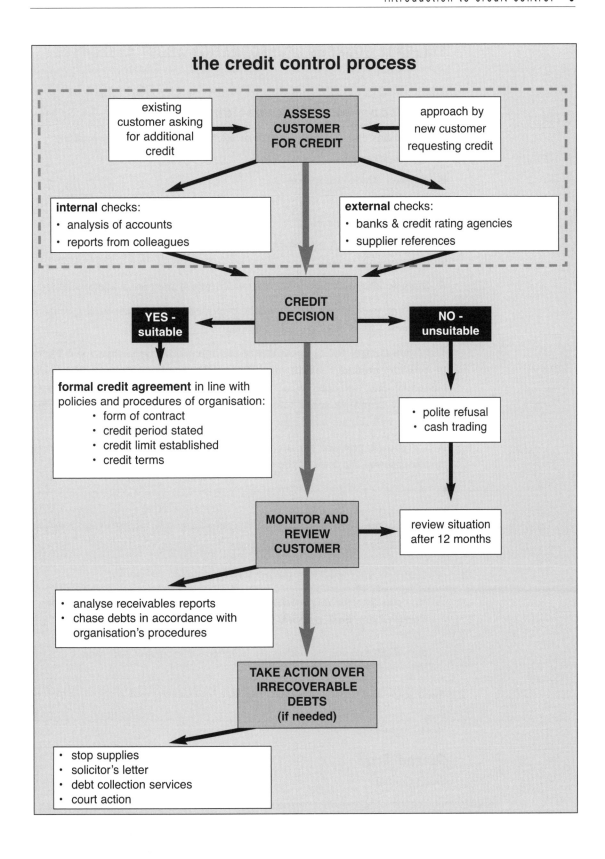

the credit control process

existing customer asking for additional credit → **ASSESS CUSTOMER FOR CREDIT** ← approach by new customer requesting credit

internal checks:
- analysis of accounts
- reports from colleagues

external checks:
- banks & credit rating agencies
- supplier references

CREDIT DECISION

YES - suitable

NO - unsuitable

formal credit agreement in line with policies and procedures of organisation:
- form of contract
- credit period stated
- credit limit established
- credit terms

- polite refusal
- cash trading

MONITOR AND REVIEW CUSTOMER

review situation after 12 months

- analyse receivables reports
- chase debts in accordance with organisation's procedures

TAKE ACTION OVER IRRECOVERABLE DEBTS (if needed)

- stop supplies
- solicitor's letter
- debt collection services
- court action

EXTERNAL SOURCES OF INFORMATION ABOUT CUSTOMERS

using sources of information

Organisations can consult a variety of sources of **external** information:

- bank references
- supplier (trade) references
- credit circles
- credit rating agencies
- accounts filed at Companies House
- official publications
- management accounts – but obviously only if they are made available

In addition, useful information can be provided by **internal** sources, ie from colleagues; this is covered in full on page 12.

The credit control policy document of the organisation (see page 13) is likely to provide guidance about establishing the creditworthiness of a new customer and indicate what external sources should be approached. Obviously common sense tells you that the size and importance of the customer will dictate what checks will need to be made.

It is common practice for an organisation to send out a letter to a new customer along the lines of the following:

Dear Sirs

Ref : Application to Open a Credit Account

Thank you for your request to open a credit account in our books.

So that I can consider your request I shall be grateful if you will supply me with:
- details of your bank account - bank, bank branch address and account name
- details (contact names, addresses, telephone numbers) of two trade references

Thank you.

Yours faithfully

Conrad Troll
Credit Control

Alternatively, the organisation may have a credit application form which it sends to customers applying for a credit account. Details might include:

- the registered name and address of a limited company, or
- the names, business and home addresses of partners, or
- the name, business and home address of a sole proprietor
- the length of time they have been in business
- any trading name used
- at least two trade references
- bank details
- credit requirement
- signature of the applicant(s)

An example is shown below.

APPLICATION FOR CREDIT

Please open a credit account in the name of ....

Address ....

....

Telephone... ....Years in business..............................

Trading name(s) where applicable ....

Amount of credit required £ .... monthly, in total £ ....

Please accept this as authority to release information to the parties below for reference purposes.

signed .... capacity .... date........................

signed .... capacity .... date........................

Bank name..

Bank address...

Trade reference 1	Trade reference 2
Name..	Name..
Address	Address ....
....	....
....	....
Tel...	Tel...

bank references

Banks have traditionally been a valuable source of information about the credit standing of prospective customers.

One problem with bank references is the language in which they are written. Banks are experts at understatement. Just as school reports need interpretation – eg 'she is a quiet student' means 'she is asleep most of the time' or 'she is lively in class' means 'she talks incessantly' – so bank reports also need interpretation.

A request for a bank reference is normally worded along the lines of:

'Do you consider Dodgee Builders Limited to be good for the figure of £50,000 trade credit per month?'

The replies that might be received are shown below, both in bank language and also in plain ordinary English. The replies are listed from top to bottom in order of creditworthiness.

bank reply	plain ordinary English
'Undoubted.'	'A good risk for the figure quoted.'
'Good for your figure and purpose.'	'A reasonable risk and most probably OK.'
'Should prove good for your figures and purpose.'	'Not so sure about this one - well worth investigating further before making a decision.'
'Although their capital is fully employed we do not consider the directors would enter into a commitment they could not see their way to fulfil.'	'This business has cash flow problems and should not be allowed any credit.'

When translated into plain English, bank references are limited but useful indicators of the prospective customer's creditworthiness.

trade references

It is common practice for organisations to ask for two trade references when assessing a customer's credit risk. These are not always reliable because the prospective customer might give as references suppliers who are not strict about credit control, and avoid quoting the suppliers who are red hot in chasing debts.

A standard letter asking for information from a trade referee is shown below.

Fine Dowt Limited

88 Station Road

Newtown NT6 9GH

Tel 01707 767188 Fax 01707 767022 www.finedowt.co.uk

Credit Control Manager
Esloy Engineering
Unit 16 Forest Estate
Bath BA2 4JP

We have received a request for credit from our customer Parsons Printers. They have quoted you as referee. We shall be grateful if you could answer the following questions.

How long have you been trading with the customer?   ....years .... months

Terms granted   amount per month £....................

Total limit   £..

Period of credit granted   ....

Payment record (please indicate as appropriate)   prompt / occasionally late / often late

Have you ever suspended credit?   Yes / No   When?...............................

Other relevant information ....

....

Thank you for your assistance. We will be happy to reciprocate at any time.

Yours faithfully

N Igmer

Nigel Igmer, Credit Controller

A reply to a trade reference may take a long time to process. The enquiring organisation can avoid delay by telephoning the enquiry to the 'sales ledger' staff after sending off the credit enquiry letter.

credit circles

An alternative adopted by some businesses is not to make the trade enquiry through the quoted referees but to telephone one of their own competitors (who are likely to deal with the customer) and speak to the sales ledger staff directly and informally – often receiving a very honest appraisal. This arrangement is known as a **credit circle**, ie a group of businesses in the same trade who exchange information about customers they have in common, and particularly those who may be experiencing cash flow problems.

credit reference agencies

Organisations which frequently process new applications for credit often subscribe to **credit reference agencies**. These are commercial organisations which offer an online service for checking the credit rating of companies and individuals. They have extensive databases which provide a wealth of material which can be provided on demand, enabling an instant credit decision to be made. They do, of course, charge for the service, and there is the risk that some of the information may be out of date. Examples include:

- **Dun & Bradstreet** (www.dnb.com)
- **Experian** (www.experian.co.uk)
- **Equifax** (www.equifax.co.uk)

Reference enquiries can be made either on limited companies or on individuals.

Reports from credit reference agencies on **limited companies** will provide details such as:

- three years' accounts
- payment history
- directors details
- any insolvency proceedings

Credit reference agencies are widely used for providing reports on **individuals** for organisations such as banks, credit card and hire purchase companies. Sole trader and partnership businesses are enterprises run by individuals. These reports will not produce much in the way of financial data (only limited companies have to file their accounts) but will provide information such as:

- names and addresses
- credit risk – based on any default on credit (including not paying credit card bills on time)
- county court judgements for non-payment of debt
- bankruptcy orders

Reports on individuals can be requested to check up on the credit rating of directors of limited company customers. A director with a bad credit record can often be found to be running a company which is also a poor credit risk.

Companies House

Another source of information about limited companies is Companies House, the Government agency to which all larger limited companies are obliged by law to send their annual accounts and to which all companies send information about directors (www.companieshouse.gov.uk).

This data is publicly available (at a cost), but financial data may not be completely up-to-date, as many companies file accounts well after the balance sheet date.

other published sources

If a credit control department wishes to find out about the creditworthiness of a large organisation it may find references and articles in the press, trade journals and online. The internet is a powerful tool here. Try doing a search on a well-known company name in Google, for example, and see what information and up-to-date news articles are produced.

management accounts

An important element of the assessment of the customer risk is analysis of the customer's **management accounts**, if they are available. This will involve the use of **performance indicators** to analyse past and up-to-date financial statements of the customer. If up-to-date financial statements are not available, draft accounts or internal management reports should be requested for analysis. Ideally, at least three years' accounts should be analysed in order to show the trends in three key areas:

- **liquidity** – the ability of the business to repay debts as they fall due
- **profitability** – the ability of the business to maintain its capital and to provide funds for repayment of debts in the future
- **gearing** – the financial risk taken on by the business shown by comparing interest bearing liabilities and total capital employed

This area of assessment and the use of **credit scoring** are covered in full in the next chapter.

INTERNAL SOURCES OF INFORMATION ABOUT CUSTOMERS

External sources of information are often used when the individual or organisation applying for credit is not known to the enquirer. If an organisation needs to assess the credit risk of an existing customer – eg when an increase in credit limit is requested – much of the information needed may already be available within the organisation. This **internal** information includes:

■ internal conversations and emails between colleagues

■ records of meetings and visits by employees of the organisation – eg by sales ledger and sales teams

internal records

Suppose two existing company customers (A and B), each with a credit limit of £10,000 ask for an increase to £15,000 because of increased trading. The credit control staff could make enquiries within the organisation . . .

Company A: **Go-A-Head Limited**	**Company B:** **Going-to-the-Wall Limited**
feedback from sales ledger team	**feedback from sales ledger team**
'Yes, they always pay on time. Never go over their limit. No problems there.'	'Not sure. They always seem to be up to their limit or slightly over. The money comes in, but it is often late, and we have had to send out chasers.'
feedback from the sales team	**feedback from the sales team**
'Yes, we went to see them last month. They seem well-organised and there is a good market for their product. They are well positioned for expansion. They find our prices very competitive. They are good to do business with.'	'We asked to visit them, but they didn't seem keen. They have a high turnover of staff – we always seem to be dealing with someone different. I personally think that they have been over-ordering from us as I am not sure that their sales are up to target. I wonder if they need the higher limit to help fund their liquidity?'
conclusion of credit control team	**conclusion of credit control team**
'On the face of it a good credit risk, but we will need to see their accounts.'	'There appear to be problems here, so we will need to see their accounts. We may struggle to recover what is owed!'

THE ORGANISATION'S CREDIT CONTROL PROCEDURES

It is important to appreciate that the credit assessments explained in the text of this chapter are likely to form part of the organisation's credit control procedures, often set down in a formal written policy document.

Where there is such a document, there will be operational requirements, set terms, standard documents, all of which will ensure that the administration of credit control runs smoothly and in line with the organisation's 'standard' procedures.

Another reason that standard procedures have to be followed is a legal one. The relationship between seller and buyer is one of contract, ie legal agreement.

If that contract is broken – eg the buyer does not pay up – the seller may need to take the buyer to court. The law is very particular and if the seller is to be successful, it is very important that all the procedures have been carried out 'to the letter'. This is particularly important in relation to terms of payment. This issue will be dealt with in full in Chapter 6.

Set out below is an example of a typical Credit Control Policy Document. Note that the Sales Department – who will be dealing with the customer on a day-to-day basis – will need to be notified of any default procedures.

CREDIT POLICY & PROCEDURES

New Accounts

1 One bank reference and two trade references required.

2 Analysis of minimum of three years' accounts for limited company customers.

Credit Terms

3 Standard terms 30 days from invoice. Any extension to be authorised by Credit Controller.

4 2.5% settlement discount at Credit Controller's discretion.

Debt Collection

5 Invoices despatched on day of issue.

6 Statements despatched first week of the month.

7 Receivables analysis produced and analysed first week of the month.

8 Reminder letter sent first week of the month for accounts 30 days overdue (Letter 1).

9 Telephone chaser for accounts 45 days overdue. Meeting arranged if required.

10 Customer on stop list if no payment received within 15 days of telephone chaser (unless meeting arranged). Sales Department notified.

11 Letter threatening legal action and stop list notification sent if payment not received within 30 days of first letter (Letter 2).

12 Legal proceedings set in motion if payment not received within 30 days of Letter 2 – subject to authorisation by Finance Director and notification of Sales Manager.

Chapter Summary

■ Sufficient liquidity in an organisation – its ability to meet immediate liabilities – is critically important because it will help to ensure that it remains solvent.

■ An effective credit control policy is essential in an organisation if liquidity is to be maintained. The prompt receipt of payments from receivables and the avoidance of irrecoverable debts are its key objectives.

■ The extent of the credit control function depends on the size of the organisation. The same basic functions will be carried out:
 – assessing applications for new credit from new customers
 – assessing applications for increased credit from existing customers
 – monitoring the sales ledger
 – chasing overdue debts
 – dealing with irrecoverable debts

■ Organisations use a variety of external sources and internal sources to provide information when assessing credit risks. External sources are likely to be used more for new customers and internal sources for existing customers.

■ External sources include bank references, trade references, credit circles, credit rating agency reports, available accounts and other publications. Some organisations ask the customer to complete a credit application form which will provide the data it needs.

■ Internal sources of information include records of meetings, conversations and visits by a variety of employees of the organisation, including the sales ledger staff and sales force.

■ Another valuable exercise in credit assessment is the ratio analysis of financial accounts – preferably from three consecutive years. This will provide information about the trends in:
 – liquidity
 – profitability
 – the financial position

■ An organisation's credit control policy will often be formalised in a written Credit Policy document which ensures that all procedures are carried out correctly.

Key Terms

liquidity	a measure of the extent to which a person or organisation has cash – or can raise cash – to meet immediate and short-term liabilities
credit control	the process of managing customers who pay on credit so that settlement of debt is made on time
bank reference	a credit report given by the customer's bank to the supplier; the information is reliable but requires some interpretation
trade reference	a credit report authorised by the customer and given by an organisation which already provides the customer with credit facilities; this information may not be as reliable as a bank reference
credit circle	a group of businesses in the same trade who exchange information about the creditworthiness of customers that they have in common
credit reference agency	an organisation which provides a wide variety of credit data about companies and individuals on a commercial basis – often online – including financial accounts, payment histories, details of court proceedings and insolvencies; this information is very detailed but can be costly
Companies House	the Government agency which holds details of all limited companies and directors; larger companies file their annual accounts at Companies House
performance indicators	the calculation of ratios from financial accounts to assess an organisation's liquidity, profitability and gearing
credit policy document	a formal document which sets down the procedures to be followed in opening new accounts, the normal credit terms and the way in which debts are collected

Activities

1.1 Liquidity management is important in a limited company business because:

(a)   it ensures that shareholders should always receive a dividend

(b)   it ensures that the company should be able to meet its short-term liabilities

(c)   it ensures that the company should be able to meet its long-term liabilities

(d)   it ensures that the company should always make a profit

Which **one** of these options is correct?

1.2 Credit control is a process which manages:

(a)   the accounts of the trade receivables of an organisation

(b)   the accounts of the trade payables of an organisation

(c)   the bank accounts of an organisation

(d)   the short-term investments of an organisation

Which **one** of these options is correct?

1.3 Possible sources of information about a potential new credit customer include:

(a)   colleagues, trade references, other customers

(b)   bank references, other customers, credit circles

(c)   trade references, colleagues, credit rating agencies

(d)   Companies House, credit rating agencies, HM Revenue & Customs

Which **one** of these options is correct?

1.4 An application form issued to a company customer requesting trade credit is likely to ask for:

(a)   the amount of credit required, VAT registration number, details of trade references

(b)   the amount of credit required, bank name and address, details of trade references

(c)   the amount of credit required, bank account number, the names of the directors

(d)   the amount of credit required, aged trade receivables analysis, names of directors

Which **one** of these options is correct?

1.5   Information about a limited company customer received from a credit reference agency can include:

(a)   financial accounts, payment history, directors' credit card numbers

(b)   financial accounts, payment history, directors' names and addresses

(c)   financial accounts, trade references, directors' names and addresses

(d)   financial accounts, trade references, bank references

Which **one** of these options is correct?

1.6   You are assessing an application for a credit limit of £15,000 from a new customer, Archway Supplies Limited. You have received the bank reference and two trade references shown below.

You are to read the references, assess them for risk and complete the table on the next page. Note that you are asked to identify the significant word in each reference which has guided your decision.

Centro Bank PLC

status report: Stylo Limited

Request: £15,000 trade credit per month

Report: Should prove good for your figure and purpose.

Response to trade credit enquiry, received from B Ruckner Ltd

Re: Stylo Limited: £15,000 trade credit per month

We have been trading with this company for five years and allow £10,000 credit per month on 60 day terms. The company normally meets its commitments on time.

Response to trade credit enquiry, received from V Williams & Co

Stylo Limited: £15,000 credit per month

We allow this customer £5,000 credit per month on 60 day terms. The account is usually paid on time.

Reference received	Risk rating			Significant word
	high ✔	medium ✔	low ✔	
Centro Bank Limited				
B Ruckner Ltd				
V Williams & Co				

1.7 You work for GML Importers Limited, an importer of toys from the Far East. The Credit Control Manager has received a letter from Toppo Toys Limited which operates a chain of 20 shops in the London area. Toppo Toys wishes to purchase stock from GML Importers Limited and is requesting credit facilities.

The company Credit Policy Manual states that to assess any new proposition you will initially need a banker's reference and two trade references.

You are to answer questions (a) and (b) on the next page.

Toppo Toys Limited

71 Clerkenwell Avenue London EC1R 5BC

Tel 0207 8371199 Fax 0207 8371192 Email sales@toppotoys.co.uk

J Root, Credit Control Manager
GML Importers Limited
29 The Greenway
Slough SL2 7GH   5 August 20XX

Dear Mr Root,

Request for credit facilities

We have purchased stock from you over the last six months and would now be grateful if you could consider providing us with credit facilities. We would initially be looking for a facility of £10,000 on thirty days terms.
As we have been trading with you on a cash terms basis for six months we hope that this can be arranged with the minimum of formality.
We look forward to hearing from you.

Yours sincerely

D Warner

David Warner
Manager

(a) Indicate whether the following statements are true or false.

	True ✔	False ✔
You will be happy to provide the credit facilities straightaway because the company is already trading with you on a cash basis		
You will only need to obtain one trade reference		
You will need a bank reference and two trade references		

(b) A bank reference, if requested, will include certain details (tick the correct option):

	✔
(a) The bank name and address and the bank account balance of the business that is requesting the credit	
(b) The bank branch address and sort code	
(c) The bank branch address and account name	

1.8 Management accounts are useful in the assessment of a company's credit standing because they provide information about (tick the correct option):

	✔
(a) liquidity, profitability, gearing	
(b) liquidity, profitability, share value	
(c) profitability, gearing, insurance cover	
(d) profitability, insurance cover, gearing	

2 Financial analysis of customer accounts

this chapter covers...

The last chapter outlined the need for an organisation granting credit to obtain and analyse the financial accounts of:

■ *a prospective new business customer, or*

■ *an existing business customer*

It is possible that your assessment will involve a detailed analysis of this type and so a study of this chapter should be seen as useful preparation for your assessment.

This analysis involves the business obtaining the financial statements of the customer and carrying out the calculation of performance indicators.

The performance indicators normally required include:

■ *liquidity indicators*

■ *profitability indicators*

■ *financial position indicators, ie levels of borrowing and equity*

■ *EBITDA (operational profitability) indicators*

Your assessment is likely also to require you to apply a credit scoring system to the performance indicators calculated.

This credit scoring system will give a numerical value to the results of the performance indicators and the total of these values will then indicate the level of credit risk shown by the financial statements.

ANALYSING CUSTOMER ACCOUNTS

As we have seen in the last chapter, feedback from within the organisation is a valuable source of information for credit assessment. It is essential that it is backed up wherever possible by an analysis of past and up-to-date financial statements of the customer. If up-to-date financial statements are not available, draft accounts or internal management reports should be requested for analysis.

As you will appreciate this requirement will be more appropriate for the larger customers who prepare these types of accounts. Ideally, at least three years' accounts should be analysed in order to show the trends in three key areas:

- **liquidity** – the ability of the business to repay debts as they fall due
- **profitability** – the ability of the business to maintain its capital and to provide funds for repayment of debts in the future
- **gearing** – the financial risk taken on by the business shown by comparing interest bearing liabilities and total capital employed

You may well be familiar with the analysis of performance indicators from your other studies. If you are unsure about this subject, you are recommended to study Osborne Books' *Financial Statements Tutorial*, Chapter 7, 'Interpretation of financial statements'.

performance indicators – important note

Occasionally there may be differences between the formulas for performance indicator ratios used in AAT Units. Gearing is an example. This does not mean that these are errors – it reflects the fact that indicators are only indicators and they also vary in commercial practice.

what is a good indicator?

The question is often asked: what is a 'good' current ratio or a 'good' liquid capital ratio? The answer is that it is impossible to give a reliable answer. Businesses vary widely in the way their assets and liabilities are structured. There are some guidelines on the next two pages shown as notes, but they should be used for guidance only. We explain **credit scoring** as a method of assessing credit risk in terms of performance indicators on page 28.

liquidity indicators

These indicators show the ability of the business to repay short-term debt from liquid or semi-liquid assets, and also to turn over its current assets such as inventory and trade receivables.

INDICATOR	FORMULA	WHAT IT SHOWS
current ratio	$\dfrac{\text{current assets}}{\text{current liabilities}}$	working capital expressed as a ratio - the higher the better*

* *In your assessment you need to express this ratio as the* **first number** *of the ratio, for example a current ratio of 1.5 : 1 is written as '1.5'.*

INDICATOR	FORMULA	WHAT IT SHOWS
liquid capital ('quick') ratio	$\dfrac{\text{current assets} - \text{inventory}}{\text{current liabilities}}$	a ratio comparing liquidity with short-term debts, but excluding inventory (which takes longer to turn into cash) - the higher the ratio, the better*

* *In your assessment this should be a single number, using the formula shown above.*

INDICATOR	FORMULA	WHAT IT SHOWS
accounts receivable collection period (days)	$\dfrac{\text{trade receivables} \times 365}{\text{sales revenue}}$	the **number of days** on average that it takes for a trade receivable to pay – this will depend on the nature of the business; 30 to 60 days is common
accounts payable payment period (days)	$\dfrac{\text{trade payables} \times 365}{\text{cost of sales}}$	the **number of days** on average that it takes to pay a supplier – this will usefully show how promptly the business pays its trade payables
inventory holding period (days)	$\dfrac{\text{inventory} \times 365}{\text{cost of sales}}$	the number of days on average that inventory is held – this will depend entirely on the nature of the inventory; the figure should ideally not increase over time

profitability indicators

These indicators show the ability of the business to generate profit which will enable it to repay its debts in the longer term.

INDICATOR	FORMULA	WHAT IT SHOWS
gross profit margin	$\dfrac{\text{gross profit} \times 100}{\text{sales revenue}}$	profit made before deduction of expenses – this should remain steady and in line with the industry average

INDICATOR	FORMULA	WHAT IT SHOWS
operating profit margin	$\dfrac{\text{profit from operations x 100}}{\text{sales revenue}}$	profit made before deduction of tax and interest – *this should remain stable*
profit for the period margin	$\dfrac{\text{profit x 100}}{\text{sales revenue}}$	profit made after deduction of all expenses – *this should ideally increase over the years, and not fall*
interest cover	$\dfrac{\text{profit before interest \& tax}}{\text{interest}}$	the ability of a business to pay interest out of its profits (calculated as a number) – *the higher the figure the better (if the profit is negative the interest cover figure is often stated as zero)*
return on equity (or return on net assets)	$\dfrac{\text{profit x 100}}{\text{equity}}$	profit made related to the **equity** (ie the total assets minus total liabilities) – *the higher the better*
return on capital employed (ROCE)	$\dfrac{\text{operating profit x 100}}{\text{capital employed}}$	profit made related to the **capital employed** by the company (the total equity + the non-current liabilities) – *the higher the better*

financial position

Financial position measures the strength and long-term financing of a company. The proportion of debt to capital is known as **gearing**. This shows the extent to which the company is financed by debt. There are two main ways in which to calculate gearing. Note that 'total debt' in the two formulas includes short-term debt as well as long-term debt. **Short-term debt** is borrowing on which interest is paid, a bank overdraft being a common example. Trade payables are **not** included in short-term debt (even though interest is sometimes charged on late payments).

As you will see below, the difference between the formulas is the inclusion of external debt with equity on the bottom line of the **first formula**. This is probably the more common formula.

gearing	$\dfrac{\text{total debt x 100}}{\text{total debt + equity}}$	the extent to which the business is funded by debt – *the higher the figure, the less secure the company*

gearing (alternative formula)	total debt x 100 / total equity	the relationship between total debt and equity but not including long-term debt as capital
short-term debt ratio	short-term debt x 100 / total debt	the reliance on short-term debt by a business – the lower the better because a reliance on short-term debt means the business will be less liquid

EBITDA – operational profitability

EBITDA stands for:

Earnings **B**efore **I**nterest, **T**ax, **D**epreciation and **A**mortisation

EBITDA is calculated by adding back the **ITDA** deductions in the Statement of Profit or Loss to the bottom-line net income. It gives an indication of the **operational profitability** of a business, ie profitability from its **day-to-day normal trading activities**, ignoring finance costs, tax and depreciation.

EBITDA is a very broad indication of the company's ability to generate cash from operations – it represents its 'cash profits'. Note that 'amortisation' is the writing off of an intangible asset or a liability, over a specified period of time (the useful life of the intangible asset or the repayment period of the liability). There are three main EBITDA ratios:

EBITDA interest cover	EBITDA / interest payable	the ability of a business to pay the interest on debt (as shown in the Statement of Profit or Loss) – the higher the figure, the lower the risk
EBITDA to interest paid	EBITDA / interest paid	the ability of the business to pay cash interest (shown in the Statement of Cash Flows) nb: this may differ from the EBITDA/interest payable figure – the higher the figure, the lower the risk
EBITDA to total debt	EBITDA / total debt	a measure of the size of the 'cash profits' in relation to the total debt – the higher the figure, the lower the risk

credit assessment – the three main criteria

- **liquidity** – does the business have sufficient short-term resources to repay debt?
- **profitability** – does the business have the longer-term ability to generate cash to repay debt? (this can also involve EBITDA)
- **financial position** – how much debt is there already in relation to the capital resources of the company?

The Case Study which follows shows the credit assessment process in action and places performance indicators in the context of the other enquiries that need to be made when assessing a customer. The chapter will then continue with a second Case Study explaining how credit scoring may be applied to the performance indicator results.

Case Study

FIRTH ELECTRONICS – CREDIT ASSESSMENT

situation

You work in the credit control section of Firth Electronics. You have been approached by a new customer, Bridge Trading Limited for credit of £10,000 a month. You have sent out your normal enquiries – a bank credit status request and two trade credit reference requests. Bridge Trading have also sent you their last three years' accounts for you to analyse. The replies and accounts summary are shown below.

You have been asked to prepare notes summarising your assessment of this company.

National Bank PLC

status report: Bridge Trading Limited

Request: £10,000 trade credit per month

Report: Good for your figure and purpose

Response to trade credit enquiry, received from A Jones & Co

Re: Bridge Trading Limited: £10,000 trade credit per month

We have been trading with this company for five years and allow £15,000 credit per month on 30 day terms. The company can sometimes take longer to pay than allowed by these terms.

Response to trade credit enquiry, received from A Patel

Bridge Trading Limited, £10,000 credit per month

We allow this customer £5,000 credit per month on 60 day terms. The account is usually paid on time, although sometimes payment can be late. The figure you quote is higher than the credit given by us but we know of no reasons why this customer should not be able to fulfil its liabilities.

SUMMARY OF FINANCIAL ACCOUNTS: BRIDGE TRADING LIMITED

	Year 1 £000	Year 2 £000	Year 3* £000
Sales revenue	1,000	1,200	1,400
Cost of sales	600	800	1,000
Current assets	440	520	600
Current liabilities**	310	355	375
Inventory	200	220	280
Trade receivables	204	230	254
Trade payables	150	161	195
Profit from operations	80	94	112
Interest paid	20	34	32
Net profit	60	60	80
Long-term debt	200	200	250
Equity	400	460	520

* Year 3 was last year and the accounts were made up to 31 December.

** Current liabilities include short-term debt and trade payables only.

solution

You process the data from the bank report, the two trade references and the three years' accounts, and set out the results in the table shown on the next page.

Note: you have been asked to calculate gearing on the total debt/(total debt + equity) basis.

ANALYSIS OF FINANCIAL ACCOUNTS: BRIDGE TRADING LIMITED

	Year 1	Year 2	Year 3
Current ratio	1.42	1.46	1.60
Liquid capital (quick) ratio	0.77	0.85	0.85
Inventory holding period	122 days	100 days	102 days
Accounts receivable collection period	74 days	70 days	66 days
Accounts payable payment period	91 days	73 days	71 days
Net profit	6%	5%	6%
Return on capital employed	13.3%	14.2%	14.5%
Interest cover	4.0 times	2.8 times	3.5 times
Gearing	47.37%	46.14%	45.26%

Note: when quoting a ratio in an assessment you should omit the ': 1' For example, you would enter '1.60' rather than '1.60 : 1'.

You draw the following conclusions:

bank report

This indicates that the bank considers Bridge Trading Limited to be a reasonable credit risk, which, as far as bank reports go, is a positive response.

trade references

Both references draw attention to the fact that Bridge Trading Limited does pay up, but is often late in doing so. The analysis of the three years' accounts will therefore need to concentrate on the liquidity ratios. Late payment can either result from inefficiency or from poor liquidity.

analysis of three years' financial accounts

The profitability ratios (net profit and return on capital employed) and gearing percentage all suggest a company with manageable debt and a consistently sound profit record. The interest cover shows an ability to cover interest costs from profit.

The current ratio and liquid capital (quick) ratio have both improved over the three years, although the current ratio does reflect a high level of trade payables (see below). The average accounts receivable collection period of 70 days shows that the business could be collecting its trade debts more efficiently. It is the accounts payable payment period that gives cause for concern, although there has been some improvement. The reason is not a lack of liquidity, but is either a conscious policy of delaying payment to help with short-term financing, or just a lack of efficiency. Firth Electronics should not accept similar delays in payment.

recommendation

Bridge Trading Limited should be allowed the credit requested, as there is sufficient liquidity in the company, but initially on 30 days' terms.

Payments should be carefully monitored and the company advised that any persistent late payments could result in withdrawal of credit and an insistence on trading on cash terms only.

USING A CREDIT SCORING SYSTEM

Credit scoring is a system which give a numerical value to the results of the performance indicators calculated and the **total** of these values then indicates the **level of credit risk** shown by the financial statements. Normally a high score will indicate a low risk, and a low score a high risk. An example of a typical scoring system is shown below and explained on the next page.

CREDIT RATING (SCORING) SYSTEM	Score
Profit from operations margin	
Losses	–5
Less than 5%	0
5% and above but less than 10%	5
10% and above but less than 20%	10
20% and above	20
Interest cover	
No cover	–30
Less than 1	–20
More than 1 but less than 2	–10
More than 2 but less than 4	0
4 and above	10
Current ratio	
Less than 1	–20
Between 1 and 1.25	–10
Between 1.26 and 1.5	0
Above 1.5	10
Gearing (total debt/(total debt plus equity))	
Less than 25%	20
25% and above but less than 50%	10
More than 50% less than 65%	0
Between 65% and 75%	–20
Between 76% and 80%	–40
Above 80%	–100
Risk	**Aggregate score**
Very low risk	Between 60 and 21
Low risk	Between 20 and 1
Medium risk	Between 0 and –24
High risk	Between –25 and –50
Very high risk	Above –50

how to work out the score

It is possible that you will be asked in your assessment to process the performance indicators you have calculated to provide a credit score which will in turn indicate the level of credit risk shown by the accounts.

As you will see from the example shown on the previous page, the credit scoring system is set out in a table subdivided into sections for:

- the margin for the profit from operations (operating profit)
- interest cover
- current ratio
- gearing

In this way the credit scoring system covers all the main areas of concern: profitability, liquidity and gearing.

Let us assume we have already worked out the performance indicators results for two very contrasting businesses: Dodgee Ltd and Sound Ltd.

1   These are entered in the table below under the heading 'result'.

2   Using the table on the previous page we obtain a score (right-hand column) for each performance indicator required and apply it to the results in the table below and write it in the appropriate score column.

3   The score columns are totalled.

4   The scores are related to the 'aggregate score' section at the bottom of the credit score table on the opposite page and the level of risk identified.

5   The level of risk is entered on the bottom line of the table below. Sound Ltd has clearly done rather better than Dodgee Ltd.

Important note: this table has been set up in this text to illustrate the **method** of credit scoring you will need to adopt. If it is not provided in your assessment, you will find a format like this a useful way of organising your data.

	Dodgee Ltd		Sound Ltd	
performance indicator	*result*	*score*	*result*	*score*
Profit from operations margin	2%	0	10%	10
Interest cover	0.5	−20	5	10
Current ratio	0.75	−20	2.0	10
Gearing	70%	−20	25%	10
Total score		−60		40
Result		Very high risk		Very low risk

shortcomings of credit scoring

It should be pointed out that not all accounts will be credit scored in this way. In fact it is a rather arbitrary way of making a judgement of credit risk as it does not take in the other opinions that can be obtained from credit references given by banks, traders and other sources. For example it may be that you find out from the press that Sound Ltd (see the example on the previous page) is a major supplier to a manufacturer that has gone into liquidation. This could have a major effect on its future liquidity. Credit scoring would not tell you that.

There now follows a Case Study which covers the whole process of calculating performance indicators and credit scoring the results.

Case Study

IPEX LIMITED:
CREDIT ASSESSMENT AND CREDIT SCORING

situation

You work in the credit control section of Ipex Limited which uses a credit rating (scoring) system to assess the credit status of new and existing customers.

You have been asked to carry out three tasks on the last two years' accounts of Kennedy Enterprises Ltd, a new customer that has requested a £50,000 credit limit.

1 Calculate the performance indicators shown in the table below, using the financial data shown on the next page for both Year 2 and Year 1. You are to complete the 'Indicator' column below as appropriate.

2 Calculate the credit score on the basis of the table on page 32. You are to complete the 'Score' column below as appropriate.

3 State the level of risk shown by the credit score.

Kennedy Enterprises Limited	Indicator Year 2	Score Year 2	Indicator Year 1	Score Year 1
Operating profit margin %				
Interest cover				
Current ratio				
Gearing %				
Total score				

Accounts for Ipex Limited (extracts)	Year 2	Year 1
Statement of profit or loss	*£'000*	*£'000*
Sales revenue	18,000	16,000
Cost of sales	12,500	12,000
Gross profit	5,500	4,000
Distribution costs	1,700	1,700
Administration costs	1,200	1,200
Profit from operations	2,600	1,100
Interest payable	500	500
Profit on ordinary activities before taxation	2,100	600
Tax on profit on ordinary activities	700	200
Profit for the financial year	1,400	400
Statement of financial position	**Year 2**	**Year 1**
	£'000	*£'000*
Non-current assets		
Tangible assets	9,000	7,800
Current Assets		
Inventories	2,400	2,000
Trade Receivables	1,400	1,200
Cash	800	800
	4,600	4,000
Payables amounts falling due within one year		
Trade payables	3,000	2,600
Net current assets	1,600	1,400
Non-current liabilities		
Long-term loans	5,000	5,000
Net assets	5,600	4,200
Equity		
Share capital	200	200
Retained earnings	5,400	4,000
Shareholders' funds	5,600	4,200

CREDIT RATING (SCORING) SYSTEM	Score
Profit from operations margin	
Losses	−5
Less than 5%	0
5% and above but less than 10%	5
10% and above but less than 20%	10
20% and above	20
Interest cover	
No cover	−30
Less than 1	−20
More than 1 but less than 2	−10
More than 2 but less than 4	0
4 and above	10
Current ratio	
Less than 1	−20
Between 1 and 1.25	−10
Between 1.26 and 1.5	0
Above 1.5	10
Gearing (total debt/(total debt plus equity))	
Less than 25%	20
25% and above but less than 50%	10
More than 50% less than 65%	0
Between 65% and 75%	−20
Between 76% and 80%	−40
Above 80%	−100
Risk	**Aggregate score**
Very low risk	Between 60 and 21
Low risk	Between 20 and 1
Medium risk	Between 0 and −24
High risk	Between −25 and −50
Very high risk	Above −50

solution

Tasks 1 and 2

Ipex Limited	Indicator	Score	Indicator	Score
	Year 2	*Year 2*	*Year 1*	*Year 1*
Operating profit margin %	14.44%	10	6.88%	5
Interest cover	5.2	10	2.2	0
Current ratio	1.53	10	1.54	10
Gearing %	47.17%	10	54.35%	0
Total score		40		15

Task 3

The higher the total score, the lower the credit risk of the possible new customer, Kennedy Enterprises Ltd.

The Year 2 (latest year) credit score is 40, which indicates a very low credit risk.

The Year 1 (previous year) credit score is 15, which indicates a low credit risk.

The credit risk has therefore improved over the two years, which is an excellent result. If all the other enquiries (eg bank and trade references) prove acceptable, Ipex Ltd should have no credit risk problems with Kennedy Enterprises Ltd and will be able to go ahead and offer appropriate credit terms, for example the requested £50,000 limit on 30 days terms.

IDENTIFYING OVERTRADING

what is overtrading?

Overtrading is the situation where a business expands its level of sales and then finds it has a shortage of working capital and not enough cash available to support that increased level of sales.

It is important for the credit controller to be able to recognise the signs of overtrading by a customer or a prospective customer. This is done by monitoring and analysing financial information and the key performance indicators.

Overtrading can occur when a business expands rapidly: increased sales requires more inventory and creates a higher level of receivables. The increased value of payables does not compensate for this and so the amount of cash is reduced. This is illustrated in the Case Study on the next page.

STRAPT-4-CASH LIMITED: OVERTRADING

Strapt-4-Cash Limited, used to be a well-run family business run by the Adams family. At the end of the year it had a working capital of £180,000. The situation changed when the Managing Director, John Adams, retired in January and his son Denver took over his post and the running of the business. He immediately set about increasing sales by cutting prices and taking on more sales reps.

As a result, sales, inventories, trade receivables and trade payables all increased by 50%. Unfortunately there were no further resources available for working capital, which remained at £180,000, as shown by the two sets of figures below:

	before £	**after £**
Inventory	100,000	150,000
Trade receivables	140,000	210,000
Bank	40,000	(30,000)
Less trade payables	(100,000)	(150,000)
Working Capital	180,000	180,000

The old Managing Director, John Adams, was unpleasantly surprised on a visit to the company to see that the bank account, which was previously kept well in credit was now £30,000 overdrawn. He spotted that trade payables had increased to £150,000 with a number of those accounts overdue and demanding payment. He also noted that credit control had become lax and receivable accounts were not paying up on time. It was a classic case of overtrading and regrettably Strapt-4-Cash went into liquidation within the year.

overtrading – the warning signs

Overtrading can occur even if the business is profitable, and it can result in the business having to cease trading. These are the usual warning signs:

- rapidly increasing sales without an increase in resources (eg new capital being introduced)
- a reduction in the level of credit control, resulting in lengthening credit periods and trade receivables not paying on time, or at all
- a consequent increase in irrecoverable debts
- cash balances reducing and the bank account going overdrawn on a regular or a permanent ('hard core') basis
- suppliers not being paid on time
- profit margins falling

overtrading – remedies

A business which is overtrading can try and remedy the situation by:

- reducing sales levels to a manageable level
- managing the sales ledger accounts more effectively
- increasing resources through the introduction of fresh capital

Chapter Summary

■ A valuable exercise in credit assessment is the ratio analysis of customer financial accounts – preferably from three consecutive years. Ratio analysis will extract performance indicators relating to liquidity, profitability and the financial position. All of these will provide information about the customer's ability to repay invoices when they fall due.

Individual performance indicators are listed in the Key Terms below.

■ A technique used to assess the credit risk of an organisation is credit scoring. This applies a numerical value, known as a 'rating' or 'score' to a number of performance indicators and the total of these 'scores' is applied to a scale of risk which runs from very high risk (very low score) to very low risk (very high score).

■ Credit scoring is a useful technique, but it must be used in combination with other assessment methods, for example bank and trade references, which may reveal information and trends not shown in purely numerical analysis.

■ Overtrading is the situation where a business expands its level of sales and then finds it has a shortage of working capital and not enough cash available to support that increased level of sales. Overtrading can lead to the failure of the business as the working capital dries up.

Key Terms

liquidity indicators	performance indicators which show the extent of the liquidity of a business, ie its ability to repay short-term liabilities:	
current ratio	$\dfrac{\text{current assets}}{\text{current liabilities}}$	*working capital expressed as a ratio*
liquid capital ('quick') ratio	$\dfrac{\text{current assets} - \text{inventory}}{\text{current liabilities}}$	*a ratio comparing liquidity with short-term debts, but excluding inventory*
accounts receivables collection period (days)	$\dfrac{\text{trade receivables} \times 365}{\text{sales revenue}}$	*the number of days on average that it takes for a trade receivable to pay*
accounts payable payment period (days)	$\dfrac{\text{trade payables} \times 365}{\text{cost of sales}}$	*the number of days on average that it takes to pay a supplier*
inventory holding period (days)	$\dfrac{\text{inventory} \times 365}{\text{cost of sales}}$	*the number of days on average that inventory is held*

profitability indicators	these ratios show the ability of the business to generate the profit needed to provide liquidity:	
gross profit margin	$\dfrac{\text{gross profit} \times 100}{\text{sales revenue}}$	*profit made before deduction of expenses*
operating profit margin	$\dfrac{\text{profit from operations} \times 100}{\text{sales revenue}}$	*profit made before deduction of tax and interest*
profit for the period margin	$\dfrac{\text{profit} \times 100}{\text{sales revenue}}$	*profit made after deduction of all expenses*
interest cover	$\dfrac{\text{profit before interest and tax}}{\text{interest}}$	*the ability of a business to pay interest out of its profits*
return on capital employed (ROCE)	$\dfrac{\text{operating profit} \times 100}{\text{capital employed}}$	*profit made related to the total equity + non-current liabilities*
financial position	the extent of the reliance of the business on external debt as opposed to capital – the less dependent the business is on external financing, the better it will be able to repay its own debts:	
gearing (common formula)	$\dfrac{\text{total debt} \times 100}{\text{total debt} + \text{equity}}$	*the extent to which the business is financed by debt*
gearing (alternative formula)	$\dfrac{\text{total debt} \times 100}{\text{equity}}$	*the relationship between total debt and equity but excluding long-term debt as equity*
short-term debt ratio	$\dfrac{\text{short-term debt} \times 100}{\text{total debt}}$	*the reliance on short-term debt by a business*
EBITDA	**E**arnings **B**efore **I**nterest, **T**ax, **D**epreciation and **A**mortisation – indicators of operational profitability	
EBITDA interest cover	$\dfrac{\text{EBITDA}}{\text{interest payable}}$	*the ability of a business to pay the debt interest shown in the Statement of Profit or Loss*
EBITDA to interest paid	$\dfrac{\text{EBITDA}}{\text{interest paid}}$	*the ability of the business to pay cash interest shown in the Statement of Cash Flows*
EBITDA to total debt	$\dfrac{\text{EBITDA}}{\text{total debt}}$	*a measure of 'cash profits' in relation to total debt*

Activities

2.1 You are assessing an application for a credit limit of £20,000 from a new customer, Swordsafe Limited.

The company has provided you with a summary of its accounts for the last three years (see below).

EXTRACT FROM FINANCIAL ACCOUNTS: SWORDSAFE LIMITED			
	Year 1 £000	Year 2 £000	Year 3 £000
Sales revenue	750	781	720
Purchases	350	363	348
Current assets	360	353	375
Current liabilities	340	330	364
Short-tem debt (included in current liabilities)	120	110	115
Inventory	200	220	280
Trade receivables	88	93	95
Trade payables	58	63	62
Profit from operations	80	86	94
Interest paid	60	71	80
Profit for the period	20	15	14
Long-term debt	121	150	190
Equity	125	145	145

(a) **You are to** calculate the performance indicators listed in the left-hand column of the table on the next page for Years 1,2 and 3 and insert the figures in the appropriate columns.

Work to two decimal places, except for the gearing and the days for the collection and payment periods which should be rounded to the nearest whole number.

When entering the answer for the current ratio and liquid capital (quick) ratio, enter only the first part of the ratio and omit the ': 1' which forms the second part of the ratio.

	Year 1	Year 2	Year 3
Current ratio			
Liquid capital (quick) ratio			
Accounts receivable collection period			
Accounts payable payment period			
Profit for the period %			
Interest cover			
Gearing			

(b) **You are to** write comments on the performance indicators under the headings set out below:

LIQUIDITY

PROFITABILITY

```
┌────────────────────────────────────────────────────────────────────────────┐
│  FINANCIAL POSITION                                                         │
│                                                                            │
│                                                                            │
│                                                                            │
│                                                                            │
│                                                                            │
│                                                                            │
│                                                                            │
└────────────────────────────────────────────────────────────────────────────┘
```

(c) State whether you consider that Swordsafe Limited should be granted the requested credit limit of £20,000.

Yes ✔	No ✔

2.2 You decide to make a list of the warning signs shown by a company which is overtrading.

You are to tick the trends below which can indicate that a company is overtrading.

	✔
(a) Falling sales and no injections of capital	
(b) Trade receivables taking less time to pay their accounts	
(c) An increasing number of irrecoverable debts	
(d) Suppliers not being paid on time	
(e) Rising profitability	
(f) A decline in operating profit	
(g) A fall in the trade receivables payment period	
(h) A fall in the trade payables collection period	
(i) An increase in level of the bank overdraft	
(j) An increasing tendency for the bank account to remain overdrawn	
(k) A substantial increase in the level of sales and no injection of capital	

2.3 You work for Ipex Limited in the credit control department and have been asked to credit score two new applications for credit:

(1) De Gass Ltd is applying for a £30,000 credit limit

(2) Vangov Ltd is applying for a £50,000 credit limit

You have been given the recent management accounts for both companies. These have been summarised and are set out in the schedules shown on pages 42 and 43.

You are to:

(a) Calculate the performance indicators required by the tables set out on this page.

(b) Complete the tables with the required performance indicators.

(c) Credit score both schedules, using the credit scoring guidelines set out on the next page and completing the tables below with your results.

(d) State the level of credit risk of the two companies.

(e) State which of the two companies you would provide with credit terms.

(f) Explain the weaknesses exposed in the accounts of the company with the higher credit risk.

Customer: De Gass Limited	Indicator	Score
Operating profit margin %		
Interest cover		
Current ratio		
Gearing %		
Total score		

Customer: Vangov Limited	Indicator	Score
Operating profit margin %		
Interest cover		
Current ratio		
Gearing %		
Total score		

CREDIT RATING (SCORING) SYSTEM	Score
Profit from operations margin	
Losses	−5
Less than 5%	0
5% and above but less than 10%	5
10% and above but less than 20%	10
20% and above	20
Interest cover	
No cover	−30
Less than 1	−20
More than 1 but less than 2	−10
More than 2 but less than 4	0
4 and above	10
Current ratio	
Less than 1	−20
Between 1 and 1.25	−10
Between 1.26 and 1.5	0
Above 1.5	10
Gearing (total debt/(total debt plus equity))	
Less than 25%	20
25% and above but less than 50%	10
More than 50% less than 65%	0
Between 65% and 75%	−20
Between 76% and 80%	−40
Above 80%	−100
Risk	**Aggregate score**
Very low risk	Between 60 and 21
Low risk	Between 20 and 1
Medium risk	Between 0 and −24
High risk	Between −25 and −50
Very high risk	Above −50

Accounts for De Gass Limited (extracts)	
Statement of profit or loss	*£'000*
Sales revenue	10,000
Cost of sales	7,000
Gross profit	3,000
Distribution costs	800
Administration costs	550
Profit from operations	1,650
Interest payable	210
Profit on ordinary activities before taxation	1,440
Tax on profit on ordinary activities	475
Profit for the financial year	965
Statement of financial position	
	£'000
Non-current assets	
Tangible assets	5,500
Current assets	
Inventories	1,100
Trade receivables	950
Cash	200
	2,250
Payables amounts falling due within one year	
Trade payables	1,500
Net current assets	750
Payables amounts falling due after more than one year	
Long-term loans	1,500
Net assets	4,750
Equity	
Share capital	250
Retained earnings	4,500
Shareholders' funds	4,750

Accounts for Vangov Limited (extracts)	
Statement of profit or loss	£'000
Sales revenue	12,000
Cost of sales	10,000
Gross profit	2,000
Distribution costs	750
Administration costs	680
Profit from operations	570
Interest payable	250
Profit on ordinary activities before taxation	320
Tax on profit on ordinary activities	105
Profit for the financial year	215
Statement of financial position	
	£'000
Non-current assets	
Tangible assets	4,000
Current assets	
Inventories	2,000
Trade receivables	550
Cash	50
	2,600
Payables amounts falling due within one year	
Trade payables	2,050
Net current assets	550
Payables amounts falling due after more than one year	
Long-term loans	2,750
Net assets	1,800
Equity	
Share capital	100
Retained earnings	1,700
Shareholders' funds	1,800

3 Granting credit and setting up customer accounts

this chapter covers...

The last two chapters have described:

- *the credit assessment process which collects internal and external information about a customer who is asking for credit terms*
- *the analysis of management accounts by extracting performance indicators and using credit scoring techniques*

In this chapter we look in more detail at the next steps in the process:

- *making the decision whether or not to grant credit*
- *advising an unsuccessful applicant in a tactful way so that business is not lost*
- *setting up an account for a successful applicant requiring credit terms*

Setting up an account is a formal process establishing a legal relationship of contract between the supplier and the customer. This chapter describes:

- *general terms of supply and payment*
- *discounts – including settlement discounts*
- *payment of interest on late payment*
- *the use of credit insurance*

The credit control process is shown on the diagram on the next page. The dotted box denotes the stage that has been reached and is explained in this chapter.

The next chapter explains in detail the legal implications of a trading relationship.

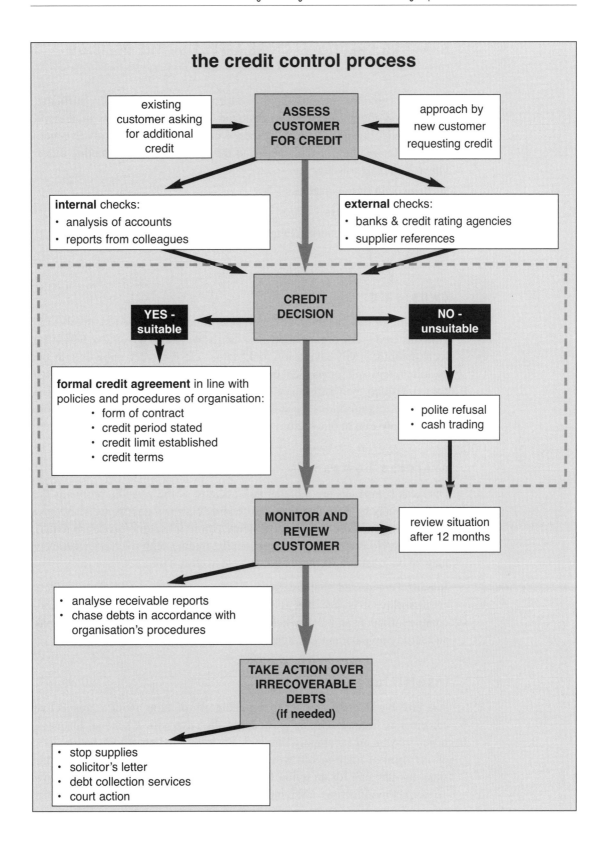

the credit control process

existing customer asking for additional credit → **ASSESS CUSTOMER FOR CREDIT** ← approach by new customer requesting credit

internal checks:
- analysis of accounts
- reports from colleagues

external checks:
- banks & credit rating agencies
- supplier references

CREDIT DECISION

YES - suitable ← → **NO - unsuitable**

formal credit agreement in line with policies and procedures of organisation:
- form of contract
- credit period stated
- credit limit established
- credit terms

- polite refusal
- cash trading

MONITOR AND REVIEW CUSTOMER → review situation after 12 months

- analyse receivable reports
- chase debts in accordance with organisation's procedures

TAKE ACTION OVER IRRECOVERABLE DEBTS (if needed)

- stop supplies
- solicitor's letter
- debt collection services
- court action

GRANTING CREDIT – FACTORS AFFECTING THE DECISION

The first chapter in this book concentrated on gathering sufficient information about a prospective customer so that a decision to grant credit can be made. It is important to appreciate that the decision will involve more than just the reading of references and the application of accounting ratios. Other factors to consider are

■ ownership of the customer

■ overseas customers

■ amount of information available

■ sales policy

ownership

Ownership of the customer will often determine the level of risk involved in granting credit. An organisation that has 'state' backing (eg the BBC or a local authority) will have a low risk status – ie it is very unlikely that the customer will fail to pay up on time. The same should be true of large companies and their subsidiary companies (which have their backing). It is the smaller organisations, eg start-up businesses, that are seen as being more risky: failure rate in this sector is higher and irrecoverable debts more likely.

overseas companies

Overseas companies are a higher risk because of the possible problems the customer may have in obtaining and sending currency payments. Also, there will be complications with legal systems should it become necessary to take court action to recover debt. Consequently, trading with overseas customers may be on a 'cash up front' basis, at least to start with.

It must be stressed that overseas customers are not seen as being less creditworthy, it is just that the logistics of obtaining payment are more complex. Banks can be very helpful in this area in advising on country risk and setting up payment guarantee schemes.

insufficient information

It is possible that the amount of available information about a prospective customer is limited. This is particularly the case with a start-up business, which may be an excellently run company with good prospects, but the lack of any form of track record will make a credit decision hard to make. This situation may call for an initial refusal of credit with a promise of a review in, say, six months time when more information will have become available.

sales policy

There can be a tension within a commercial organisation between the sales function and the credit control function. Sales staff will want to obtain as many sales leads and new customers as possible in order to meet targets, even if the credit risks involved are higher than the credit control function would normally tolerate. The decision of whether or not to grant credit may therefore be swayed by current management policy, whether it be to 'play it safe' or to 'go all out for new sales'.

REFUSING CREDIT

The decision not to grant credit is a difficult one for all concerned. The organisation taking the decision is in danger of losing business because the potential customer may well go to another supplier; the potential customer will in turn lose both a supplier and a source of liquidity (remember that credit granted by a supplier = short-term financing).

The supplier is likely to suggest to the customer that cash trading (ie immediate 'on the nail' payment) would be an alternative until the credit status of the customer is reviewed in, say, six months time.

The supplier will have to treat the matter with great tact and diplomacy. A letter should be sent to the customer explaining the situation. The letter could incorporate some of the sentences shown below and should be written to relate to the circumstances of the case.

Dear Customer

Application for trade credit

'Thank you for your letter/application form of .... requesting credit of ....'

'We have assessed your application for credit using our usual criteria and have taken up references, but very much regret that we are unable to offer credit facilities to you at present.'

'We will be happy to review the situation again in six months time, when we have seen your latest financial accounts.'

'We very much value your custom and would be very pleased to trade with you on a cash basis for the time being. Our Sales Manager, Guy Weston, would be very interested in discussing this with you. His email address is gweston@gmlimporters.co.uk'

We look forward to hearing from you.'

half-way house credit

Some organisations, anxious not to lose a customer, might compromise and agree credit terms that are 'half-way' to what the customer requested. Examples of this are:

■ shorter credit periods, eg 7 days rather than 30 days

■ part payment, eg pay 25% cash terms and 75% after 30 days

This will not remove the risk of the customer not paying, but it reduces it, and may help to retain a good customer who would otherwise have gone to another supplier.

keeping to organisational policy

It must be stressed that all credit control decisions reached, whether a 'yes' or 'no' decision, must comply with the Credit Control Policy and Procedure Document used by the organisation, an example of which was given on page 13. Another example is shown on the opposite page. Note that the 'credit terms' section of this document relates to the contents of this chapter.

CHANGES IN CREDIT TERMS

It may be that an existing customer will ask for a change in credit terms. This might be:

■ a request for an increased limit, eg from £10,000 to £15,000

■ a request for a longer payment period, eg an extension from 30 to 60 days

These may be requested with a certain amount of pressure from the customer – for example: 'Ipex Limited, who also supply me, give me 60 days' credit, and we would not want to take our business away from you.'

Whatever the circumstances, common sense and an analysis of the customer's trading history will be needed, together with a check on the Policies and Procedures requirements. In the case of a request to increase the limit, factors to examine will include:

■ the amount of the increase – is it justified? – is it enough?

■ has the customer kept within the existing limit?

■ the trading history – have invoices been paid in full and on time?

If an extension of the credit period is required, the important thing is to check out the customer's liquidity. If the customer is experiencing cash flow problems one of the first solutions is to obtain longer credit from suppliers, effectively using the supplier to finance working capital shortages.

CREDIT CONTROL POLICIES AND PROCEDURES

New Accounts

1   One bank reference and two trade references are required.

2   A credit reference agency report and the last three years published accounts for limited companies need to be analysed.

3   A credit reference agency report and the last three years accounts for a sole trader need to be analysed.

Existing customers

4   A credit reference agency report to be obtained on an annual basis together with the latest annual accounts (either from Companies' House or directly from the customer). Both documents to be reviewed.

5   A trading history review to be undertaken annually to review for performance against credit limits and terms of payments.

6   Annual review of usage of the customers credit limit to ensure that an outdated credit limit is not in existence. This is particularly important where the trade with the customer has reduced over the past year.

Credit terms

7   Standard terms are 30 days from invoice. Any extension to be authorised by the Finance Director.

8   A 2% settlement discount to be offered to all accounts with a profit margin of 50% or greater, or with a profit margin of 30% and a value in excess of £50,000 or with the credit controller's discretion.

Debt collection process

9   Invoices to be despatched on day of issue, (day of issue to be no more than 2 days after date of delivery).

10   Statements to be despatched in the second week of the month.

11   Receivables analysis to be produced and reviewed on a weekly basis.

12   Reminder letter to be sent once an account is overdue.

13   Telephone chaser for accounts 15 days overdue.

14   Customer on stop list if no payment is received within 5 days of the telephone chaser. Computerised sales order processing system updated and automatic email sent to the customer contact and the account manager (sales person).

15   Letter threatening legal action if payment not received within 30 days of the first letter.

16   Legal proceedings / debt collection agency instructed subject to the approval of the Finance Director.

17   Prepare a report suggesting an appropriate provision for irrecoverable or doubtful debts.

18   If at any stage in the process the customer is declared insolvent or bankrupt then contact the insolvency practitioner in order to register the debt and notify the financial accountant so that the VAT can be reclaimed.

OPENING A NEW ACCOUNT

When the decision to grant credit has been taken, the account should be set up without delay and advised in writing to the customer, normally in a formal letter. This document will set out, in accordance with Policies and Procedures requirements:

- the period for which credit will be made available (eg 12 months)
- the limit on the account, eg £20,000
- the credit terms, eg 30 days from date of invoice
- discounts (including any settlement discount available)
- payment details (optional)
- interest penalties for late payment

This document is an important one for legal reasons. It can be referred to in later documentation, eg conditions of sale printed on the back of an order acknowledgement or invoice, and will be binding on the purchaser in the contract of sale which is set up each time a supply is made. We will explain in more detail about contracts of sale and legislation relating to selling in the next chapter. We will first explain the terms which will be set out in the letter to the customer when the account is opened.

credit period and limit

This limit is the upper limit which will be set on the sales ledger account of the new customer for a set period of time. A 'rule of thumb' calculation is that the limit should be twice the average monthly sales expected to be made to the customer. The period of the limit is normally twelve months.

credit terms

A number of credit payment terms need explanation. Note the distinction between 'net' – which refers to the timing of the supply of goods or services – and the use of the invoice date to calculate the payment date.

cash terms	immediate payment, ie zero credit
30 days from date of invoice	payment is due 30 days after the invoice date, eg payment of an invoice dated 10 March is due by 10 April
net monthly	payment of one month's supplies of goods or services is due at the end of the following month, eg payment of a delivery dated 10 March is due by 30 April

net 30 days   payment of a supply of goods/services is due 30 days after the delivery (the same principle is applicable to 'net 60 days' etc)

discounts and interest rate comparisons

Trade discount is traditionally given to established customers who buy on a regular basis, although a new customer may be given it straightaway, particularly if it has been requested as part of a 'deal' to open the account. The amount will vary according to the product. For example, a textbook like this one may sell to a bookshop at a trade discount of around 30%.

Settlement discount (also known as cash discount) is a percentage reduction in selling price allowed when settlement is made earlier than normal, eg '2.5% discount for settlement within 7 days'. For example, a purchaser receiving an invoice for £100 (ignoring VAT) with these terms will only have to pay £97.50 (ie £100 less £2.50 discount).

Settlement discount is attractive **when interest rates are high**. This is because money that may otherwise have been borrowed on overdraft by the seller to finance working capital – at a high interest rate – will be paid into the bank earlier and the interest cost will be reduced accordingly.

Alternatively, **when interest rates are high**, the seller could invest the cash received earlier through settlement discount at an attractive interest rate.

If interest rates are low, the cost to the seller of offering settlement discount (ie the reduction in the selling price) can be comparatively high, which makes it less attractive.

The **annual equivalent** of the cost related to a **simple interest rate** can be worked out by the formula shown below. The cost is worked out on an annual equivalent basis so that it can be compared with interest rates (also quoted per annum):

$$\left[\frac{d}{100-d}\right] \times \left[\frac{365}{N-D}\right] \times \quad 100\% \quad = \quad \text{annual cost of discount}$$

Where   d   =   settlement discount percentage

        N   =   normal settlement period in days

        D   =   settlement period for early payment in days

The calculation of the **annual equivalent** of the cost related to a **compound interest rate** is more complex and the AAT recommends that students should use a suitable **scientific calculator** to perform this operation if it is required in the examination. The calculation of a **simple interest rate** comparison is shown in a worked example on the next page.

worked example – the cost of offering settlement discount

Your business is considering offering 1.5% settlement discount for payment of invoices within seven days rather than the thirty days normally offered. How much is it going to cost your business on an annual basis? How does it compare with the 8% it might cost you to finance the invoice on a bank overdraft? How does it compare with investment rates available at the time?

solution

The formula is

$$\left[\frac{d}{100-d}\right] \times \left[\frac{365}{N-D}\right] \times 100\% = \text{annual cost of discount}$$

d = settlement discount percentage   = 1.5%
N = normal settlement period in days   = 30
D = settlement period for early payment = 7

The calculation is

$$\left[\frac{1.5}{98.5}\right] \times \left[\frac{365}{23}\right] \times 100\% = \text{annual cost of discount} = 24.17\%$$

This shows that the annual cost to the business will be 24.17% which is more expensive than financing the extra 23 days (ie 30 less 7 days) on overdraft at 8% per annum. Cash discount therefore does not look like a good idea.

Also, if the business was considering investing the cash received 23 days earlier, the investment rate would need to be in excess of 24.17% to make it at all worthwhile; this is extremely unlikely.

payment details

Payment can be made in a number of different ways, and these can have a cost implication. Generally speaking, payment by cheque and cash is more expensive both for the customer and the supplier in terms of handling costs and bank charges. It is also becoming far less common.

Many organisations actively encourage computer payments through the BACS and Faster Payments systems which transfer money from one account to another by computer. When setting up an account, the seller may request electronic payments instead of cheque payment.

interest penalties for late payment

It is common practice for organisations to include in their terms and conditions the right to charge interest on late payments. Not many organisations will necessarily enforce this right, because they then run the risk of alienating and losing the customer. The terms are normally included as an incentive to pay. The extract below is taken from the terms and conditions on account opening documentation.

> Our terms are strictly 30 days after invoice date. Interest will be charged at 2% per month (or part thereof) on all amounts unpaid after the due date.

Interest on late payment is also enforceable in law, although organisations are only likely to take legal action as a very last resort. The law is the **Late Payment of Commercial Debts (Interest) Act 1998**, modified by the **Late Payment of Commercial Debts Regulations 2013**. This legislation sets out an automatic legal right to charge interest and to demand debt recovery costs.

The **interest rate** that can be charged is the Bank of England official dealing (base) rate plus 8%. The interest – worked out as a simple interest rate – is based on the amount including VAT and calculated for the period during which the payment is late. An example calculation is shown below.

worked example – the interest that can be charged on late payment of a commercial debt

Your business is owed £1,000 (plus VAT @20%). The debt is 60 days late. Bank of England base rate is 1%. The formula and calculation for interest charged for late payment is:

Interest formula: Amount including VAT x (base rate + 8%) x $\dfrac{\text{Number of days debt overdue}}{365}$

Calculation: (£1,000 + £200 VAT) x (1% + 8%) x $\dfrac{60}{365}$

= £1,200 x 9/100 x 0.16 = £17.28 interest which can be charged

retention of title (ROT)

Another term which sometimes appears on the front of invoices and in the small print on the back of sales documents is that ownership of the goods sold does not pass to the buyer until payment has been made. This is known as a **retention of title** clause or by its quaint acronym '**ROT**'.

If the buyer becomes bankrupt/insolvent, this will enable the seller to attempt to reclaim the goods and so get some value back. This is workable when the goods are easily identifiable, such as books or packets of crisps, but causes problems when the goods are raw materials, eg blank paper or potatoes.

An example of a retention of title clause is shown below:

> 5.   Title in all Goods supplied by the Company shall vest in the Company until the Company has received full payment in respect thereof.

The effect of retention of title clauses in situations of personal bankruptcy and company insolvency is explained in full on page 110.

CREDIT INSURANCE

UK sales – credit insurance

Credit insurance replaces cash lost when a debt goes bad. Specialised companies such as Euler Hermes and Coface UK offer tailor-made solutions for different types and sizes of organisation. Typical options include:

- **whole turnover insurance** – general (up to 90%) coverage in the case of trade receivable default (non-payment of debts)

- insurance limited to **key accounts** – up to 40 customers with up to 100% coverage

- **single account** insurance – 100% cover

Premiums will depend on the risk involved and the insurer will insist on credit analysis of larger customers.

Credit insurance – if it is taken – is therefore an integral part of the credit control process. Businesses may decide to insist on credit insurance for doubtful risk customers in times of recession, but they do face the danger that the insurance may be withdrawn if a particular business becomes uninsurable. The withdrawal of credit insurance played a large part in the collapse of the retail chain Woolworths.

overseas sales – export credit insurance

Businesses that sell goods and services abroad are often advised to set up **export credit insurance**. This covers:

- the **credit risk** of selling to an overseas buyer – inevitably it is more difficult to chase up overseas debts, and should the debt turn bad, it is likely to prove difficult to bring court action against the customer

- the **political risk** of selling to a country where the political situation is less stable and might produce a revolution, civil war or economic collapse, all of which would reduce the possibility of receiving payment

Export credit insurance cover is available from **private sector commercial companies** for the supply of consumer goods and services sold on credit.

Chapter Summary

■ The decision to grant credit involves a variety of different factors involving levels of risk: internal and external credit information, the nature of the ownership of the organisation, its location (UK or overseas), the amount of information available and the level of risk attached to the sales policy.

■ If credit is to be refused, the communication of the refusal to the potential customer should be carried out in a tactful and diplomatic way, and the opportunity to trade on a cash basis offered.

■ Some organisations may be willing to compromise and offer limited credit terms to a partially risky customer; these terms might include a shorter credit period or acceptance of part payment of invoices.

■ Customers may ask for a change in credit terms, for example an increase in limit or an extension in the payment period. The proposition should be viewed in the light of the amount involved and the customer's trading history.

■ When the decision to grant credit has been made, the supplier should set out the credit terms in writing for the customer. This should include:
  - the credit period
  - the credit limit
  - the payment terms
  - details of discounts
  - payment instructions
  - interest penalties on late payment

■ The granting of settlement discount is normally more cost effective when interest rates are high. The annual cost of granting the discount can be calculated by formula and compared with the current cost of borrowing, or interest rates for investing the money.

■ Penalties on late payment can be written into the credit terms as required. There is also a statutory right to claim interest on late payments under the Late Payment of Commercial Debts (Interest) Act 1998 as amended by the Late Payment of Commercial Debts Regulations 2013.

■ Sellers of goods often include a 'Retention of Title' (ROT) clause in their documentation to enable them to recover goods sold if the buyer becomes insolvent.

■ Credit insurance can be useful cover for avoiding irrecoverable debts and may be required as part of the credit control policy. It has the weakness, however, that it may be withdrawn from businesses which are experiencing severe cash-flow problems.

credit terms	the terms on which credit is made available to a customer; they will involve the credit period, amount, discounts, payment details, late payment penalties
cash terms	immediate payment, ie zero credit
net monthly	payment of a month's supplies is due at the end of the following month
net 30 days	payment of a supply of goods (or services) is due 30 days after the delivery (or performance)
settlement discount	discount given for early settlement of invoices (also known as 'cash' discount)
interest penalties	penalties charged on amounts outstanding after the due date of payment, charged at a fixed rate of interest
Late Payment of Commercial Debts (Interest) Act 1998	allows suppliers to charge interest on overdue amounts (amended by the Late Payment of Commercial Debts Regulations 2013)
retention of title	the right of a seller of goods to retain ownership of the goods until payment is made
credit insurance	insurance of the supplier of goods and services against irrecoverable debts incurred – cover available for a range of combinations of customers (eg all customers, key customers, individual customers)

Activities

3.1 A 'rule of thumb' calculation for the size of a credit limit granted to a customer is based on an amount equal to:

(a)   50% of the estimated annual sales turnover of the customer's account

(b)   50% of the amount of the turnover of the customer's account covered by credit insurance

(c)   one month's turnover of the customer's account

(d)   two months' turnover of the customer's account

Which **one** of these options is correct?

3.2 'Net monthly' terms on a credit account means that:

(a)   payment must be made within one month of the actual invoice date

(b)   payment of one month's invoices is due at the end of the following month

(c)   each month's payment is made net of deduction of settlement discount

(d)   the settlement is made online via the internet

Which **one** of these options is correct?

3.3 A business is most likely to gain an advantage from offering settlement discount for early payment of invoices when:

(a)   overdraft interest rates are high

(b)   overdraft interest rates are low

(c)   the trade discount rate is low

(d)   the trade discount rate is high

Which **one** of these options is correct?

3.4 ABC Ltd's terms of payment are 28 days. It is offering a discount of 1% for payment within 7 days. Bella Donna owes £100. The amount the customer will pay if she takes advantage of the discount, and the simple annual interest rate will be:

(a)   £97.50 and 44.57%

(b)   £99.00 and 17.38%

(c)   £99.00 and 17.56%

(d)   £98.50 and 26.47%

Which **one** of these options is correct?

3.5 Credit insurance allows a company to claim for amounts owed:

(a)   by the company to the bank when company liquidity is low

(b)   by the company's customers when their debts become irrecoverable debts

(c)   by company employees who have used company credit cards and have left the company

(d)   by the company to suppliers when a retention of title clause is operating

Which **one** of these options is correct?

3.6 The Late Payment of Commercial Debts (Interest) Act allows:

(a)   suppliers to charge interest on overdue amounts owing

(b)   banks to increase interest charged on loans when repayments are delayed

(c)   customers to delay payment of invoices when their liquidity is low

(d)   customers to delay payment of invoices when settlement discount is offered

Which **one** of these options is correct?

3.7 A retention of title (ROT) clause states that:

(a)   customers retain title to the goods supplied as long as they can be identified

(b)   customers retain title to the goods supplied until they are paid for

(c)   suppliers retain title to the goods supplied until they are paid for and can be identified

(d)   suppliers retain title to the goods supplied when they cannot be identified

Which **one** of these options is correct?

3.8 An invoice for goods supplied is dated 27 April. The goods are delivered on 2 May.

When is the invoice due for payment if the terms are:

(a)   30 days of date of invoice?

(b)   net monthly?

(c)   net 30 days?

3.9   **(a)**   What is the annual cost to an organisation of granting settlement discount of 1.5% for settlement within 30 days? The normal payment period granted is 60 days.

(b)   Would granting settlement discount be an attractive option for the seller if the cost of borrowing on overdraft was

(1)   15% p.a.

(2)   25% p.a.

Give reasons for your answers.

3.10 You work in the credit control section of RPG Limited. The company has recently received an application for £45,000 credit terms from a new customer, Artax Limited.

The normal bank and trade credit enquiries have been made and have produced a positive result.

Artax have provided two years' accounts which have been analysed and credit scored. The results of this analysis and the credit scoring ratings are shown below.

Artax Limited	Indicator Year 2	Score Year 2	Indicator Year 1	Score Year 1
Profit from operations margin %	6.97%	0	25.14%	10
Interest cover	2.2	−10	4.1	10
Current ratio	1.10	0	2.1	5
Gearing %	65.22%	−10	46.17%	10
Total score				

The internal policy documentation of RPG Limited provides the following guidelines for granting of credit based on the credit score obtained.

CREDIT SCORING RISK CRITERIA		
Total score	**Risk level**	**Action**
60 to 21	Very low	Accept
20 to 1	Low	Accept
0 to −24	Medium	Refer to Financial Director (cash trading recommended)
−25 to −49	High	Unacceptable
−50 and lower	Very high	Unacceptable

You are to:

(a) Work out the total credit score for the last two years by completing the table above.

(b) State the credit risk for Year 1 and Year 2.

(c) Recommend a course of action.

(d) Prepare the text of a suitable reply to Artax Limited.

3.11   You work in the credit control section of RPG Limited. The company has recently received an application from an existing customer, Hermes Limited, for an increase in their credit limit. The current limit is £50,000 and they wish to increase this to £90,000 following a recent period of expansion in trading by the company.

The most recent credit scoring of the accounts of Hermes Limited produced the following results:

Hermes Limited	Indicator Year 2	Score Year 2	Indicator Year 1	Score Year 1
Profit from operations margin %	15.32%	0	22.34%	10
Interest cover	2.1	−10	4.1	0
Current ratio	1.03	0	1.5	5
Gearing %	65.22%	−10	51.17%	0
Total score		−20		15

The credit score totals indicate that the credit risk level over the two years increased as follows:

Year 1:   15 credit score   = Low risk

Year 2:   −20 credit score   = Medium risk

According to the Credit Control Policies and Procedures of the company, this greater level of risk means that the request for an increase in credit limit will need to be referred to the Financial Director for approval. In order to prepare for this proposal to go to the Finance Director, you decide to:

- research your records for details of Hermes Limited's trading history
- contact Hermes Limited for more up-to-date financial data – you have noticed that the credit-scored data shown above is nearly nine months out of date

The results of your findings are as follows:

trading history
Hermes Limited, after some excesses last year, has traded within the £50,000 credit limit for the last six months. Hermes Limited always settles its account within the stipulated 30 days period.

recent financial data
The following figures were taken from the latest management accounts (£000s):

Sales revenue	2,000
Profit from operations	640
Interest payable	80
Current assets	2,600
Current liabilities	1,300
Total debt	1,750
Equity	2,000

You are to:

(a)   Complete the table below using the latest financial figures and the figures for Year 2 from the table on the previous page for your calculations.

Performance indicator	Year 2	current year
Profit from operations margin %		
Interest cover		
Current ratio		
Gearing %		

(b)   Write brief comments on the trend shown by each of the performance indicators, stating how they will reflect on the credit rating of Hermes Limited. Include a brief general conclusion stating whether or not you consider the credit limit should be increased.

(c)   Write the text of an email to your Finance Director giving your recommendation, with reasons, for the acceptance or refusal of the request for the increase in limit from £50,000 to £90,000.

4 Customer accounts – legal aspects

this chapter covers...

The last chapter described the practicalities of:

- *setting up a credit account for a customer*
- *assessing credit risk*
- *dealing with requests for an increase in a credit limit*
- *refusing credit*

You also have to know about the legal framework which governs a trading relationship. This can involve:

- *the law of contract, which has been established over the centuries between sellers and buyers and is part of common law – ie it is not set down in Acts of Parliament*
- *legislation, which is law covering specific areas such as the sale of goods and services, and is set down in Acts of Parliament*

Specific legislation covered in this chapter includes:

- *Trade Descriptions Act*
- *Sale of Goods Act*
- *Consumer Credit Act*
- *Unfair Contract Terms Act*
- *Data Protection Act*

The next chapter describes how an account is monitored, with the overall aim of reducing the incidence of irrecoverable debts.

CUSTOMERS AND CONTRACTS

Part of your studies involves the understanding of the legal framework which enables buying and selling to take place and which states what can happen if there is a dispute. The agreement between the parties is known as a **contract**.

what is a contract?

a contract is a legally binding agreement enforceable in a court of law

Contracts, which may be in writing, or by word of mouth (oral), are agreements between two parties. Examples include:

- a written contract which you sign if you issue a purchase order for goods
- an oral contract if you have a meeting with a supplier and agree to buy a certain quantity of specified goods
- an oral contract if you order goods over the telephone

In each case somebody does something for which some kind of payment is made. A contract is **an agreement with legal consequences** because if the work done is not satisfactory, or if the payment is not made, the wronged party can take the other person to court for **breach of contract.**

Contract law affects many business arrangements, including the granting of credit. For example if you quote an incorrect price to a customer, the customer may be able to hold your business to that price, under the terms of the contract of sale. If you fail to finish a job for a customer, the customer may be able to go to court to obtain a court order for your business to complete the work under the contract.

the three elements of a contract

There are three elements which are common and essential to all contracts:

elements of a contract

agreement – an offer and an acceptance

bargain – some value (consideration) passes

intention to create legal relations – the agreement is commercial

THE AGREEMENT – OFFER AND ACCEPTANCE

the offer

An **offer** may be made by:

- the **seller** of goods and services to an individual, a group, or generally to anyone who wishes to make a purchase, or . . .

- the **buyer** of goods and services who wishes to place a definite order for goods or services using a signed purchase order or an online authorisation for an online purchase

The acceptance of an offer – from the seller or the buyer – will then form the basis of a **legally binding contract** which can be upheld in a court of law. At the time the contract is formed various terms and conditions relating to price, quantity and discount can be agreed and form an integral part of the agreement (see pages 68-69).

invitation to treat

An offer is quite different from an **invitation to treat** which is an invitation to a person to make an offer. Goods on supermarket shelves, for example, are an invitation for a customer to take the goods to the checkout where the customer will – legally speaking – offer to purchase the goods at the price indicated **at the checkout**, which is where the **contract** takes place.

A business offering its goods for sale in a catalogue (paper-based or online) is also making an invitation to treat. The customer seeing the catalogue can then proceed to issue a purchase order or place the order online at the current price which will be agreed between the supplier and the customer.

---

practical example – invitation to treat

problem
Basil sees a computer advertised in the local paper for £50. He telephones the computer supplier who tells him that the figure is a printing error – it should have been £500. Basil is angry and insists on buying his computer for £50. The problem is, does a contract exist on the basis of the £50 quoted?

answer
Basil has no rights here. There is no contract because the £50 quoted is only **an invitation to treat**, an invitation for Basil to buy the computer. The company will clearly not agree to £50 for a new computer.

termination of an offer

An offer may only be accepted while it is still open for acceptance. An offer may be terminated in the following circumstances:

■ the time limit (if there is one) expires; if there is no time limit the offer lapses after a reasonable period of time

■ the offeror – the person making the offer – may revoke (cancel) the offer

■ an offer may be rejected by the making of a counter-offer; for instance, if you offer your car for sale for £1,500 and someone offers you £1,350, that is a counter-offer

■ by acceptance or rejection of the offer

acceptance of an offer

Acceptance of an offer must be firm and unambiguous; it may be in spoken words, written form or even implied by action. Acceptance cannot be assumed from silence on the part of the person to whom the offer is made. For instance, if you say "I offer you my car for £1,500; if I have not heard from you within a week I will assume the deal is done", there is no acceptance. The offeree may go on holiday, or forget it even happened.

Acceptance must also be **unconditional**. Any new term introduced – "I will agree to buy your car as long as the wing is resprayed" – amounts to a counter-offer and will revoke the original offer.

The term "**subject to contract**", often seen on estate agents' boards, means that the terms of the offer to the offeree seem satisfactory, but have not been finally accepted. The two parties involved have agreed to draw up a formal contract for signature at a later date. There is no binding contract at this point.

The rules relating to **communication of acceptance** are largely dictated by what is required by the offer:

■ the acceptance must be communicated to the person making the offer

■ if the offer requires acceptance by a specific means (letter/fax/verbal message/email) then that means must be used for the acceptance to be effective

THE BARGAIN: CONSIDERATION

A valid contract involves a bargain, a passing of value, known in law as **consideration**. If a business buys goods there is a two way process involved:

- the supplier promises to deliver the goods
- the buyer agrees to pay for them

The parties involved are the promisor, the supplier that promises to supply the goods and the promisee, the buyer who has to make payment. The **consideration** here is the 'value' given by both parties:

- the payment – the price paid by the buyer for the goods provided
- the value of the goods handed over by the seller

There are a number of legal rules which relate to consideration:

consideration must be sufficient

Consideration must by law be sufficient. This means that:

- it must have value, although the value need not be adequate in some eyes; for example, you could sell this book for 5p; many might think the amount to be inadequate, but the 5p still has value and is therefore consideration
- it must be sufficient, ie it must be in return for the promise; money due for some other reason or obligation is not sufficient consideration

consideration – other issues

The person who is promised goods or a service **must themselves provide payment** if the promise is to be enforceable as a contract. If you buy goods, you must make the payment. If someone else pays for you (an unlikely event!) you cannot take the supplier to court if the goods do not arrive.

Also, the consideration **should not happen before the promise**. If you mend someone's car without any mention of payment, and the car owner the following week promises to give you £50, and subsequently refuses to pay you, there is no contract. The promise of payment followed the service provided.

practical example – consideration

problem
Basil runs a computer maintenance business and promises to repair a computer for a friend free of charge one weekend. Unfortunately Basil wipes all the data from the computer and it cannot be replaced. His friend says he will sue Basil. Can he? Is there a contract?

answer
No. There is no contract because there is no consideration – no money has been paid. Basil has made a mistake but he cannot be sued.

THE INTENTION TO CREATE LEGAL RELATIONS

A contract is an agreement involving consideration which the parties intend to be legally binding. In other words the parties entering a contract can reasonably expect the agreement to be enforced in a court of law if the need arises. The law assumes:

■ commercial agreements are intended to be legally binding

■ social and domestic arrangements are **not** intended to be legally binding

In short, if a person enters a contract to buy your car and then, without reason, refuses to pay for it, you can take him or her to court. If you ask a friend out for the evening, promising to take him or her out for a meal, and your friend doesn't turn up, you can not take court action. The sale of a car involves the intention to create legal relations, the invitation out does not.

BREACH OF CONTRACT

A contract normally contains certain terms which must be fulfilled as part of the agreement. If a person breaks one of those terms, that person is in **breach of contract**. For example, if a supplier undertakes to supply goods, it must send the goods on the due date, and in turn expects the goods to be paid for by a certain time. If the customer does not pay, he or she is in breach of contract and may be taken to court for **damages** (money compensation).

Contract terms may be classified as follows:

express terms	explicitly stated terms which are binding on both parties to the contract
conditions	fundamental terms of the contract which, if broken, will enable the injured party to reject the contract and to go to court to sue for damages
warranties	minor terms which if broken can be cause for an action for damages for loss suffered; the contract, however, remains in force
implied terms	terms which are not stated, but which are implied by trade custom or by law; for instance, goods sold should be of "satisfactory quality", in accordance with the Sale of Goods Act

In short:

■ express terms are written into the contract; implied terms are not

■ conditions are important terms, warranties are less important

remedies for breach of contract

Legal action can be taken against a customer when a contract is in existence because non-payment is a **breach of contract** – the receivable (debtor) is not carrying out an agreed part of the contract.

There are a number of **remedies** available for breach of contract in a wide variety of situations. A common legal term used is **damages**, which is **money compensation for loss or injury.**

The actual remedy chosen will depend on the type of contract. For example, a builder who is contracted to build a house and disappears off site before putting the roof on, can be ordered by the court to complete the work – this is the remedy of **specific performance**.

If, however, the person having the house built refuses the builder access to the site for some reason or other, the builder could terminate the contract and demand payment for what had been done – this is the remedy of **quantum meruit**, which means 'what it deserves'. In other words, the law assumes a promise made by the employer to the builder that he will pay him for his work, as much as he may deserve or merit.

These situations do not have much relevance to credit control in an organisation. Here the remedy of **action for the price** – ie taking legal action in the courts for recovery of an unpaid debt – is the normal remedy for breach of contract involving a customer who refuses to pay up.

TERMS OF COMMERCIAL CONTRACTS

It is normal business practice for the seller to make sure that when goods or services are sold that the **terms and conditions of sale** – ie the price and payment terms – are clearly set out in the contract granting credit. If there is then any problem, late payment or non-payment for example, the supplier can hold the customer to the stated terms, in a court of law if necessary.

These terms are often printed on the back of the order acknowledgement or invoice issued by the supplier, as in the example extract shown on the next page. The terms here include:

1   the supplier's terms take precedence over the customer's terms

2   the supplier is not bound by prices in the catalogue (this is a reinforcement of the fact that these prices are an invitation to treat)

3   the supplier can ask for references and also cancel a credit limit if needed

4   payment is to be made on 30 days from date of invoice terms

5   retention of title clause (see page 53)

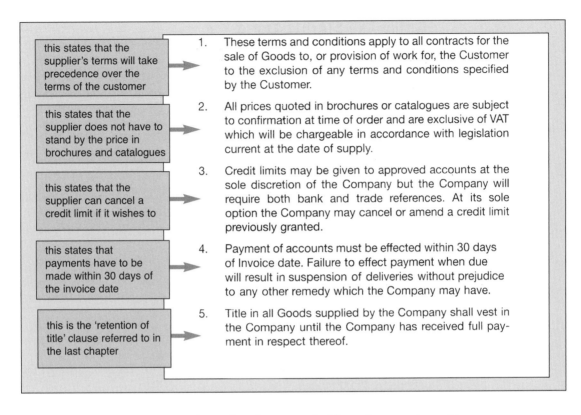

this states that the supplier's terms will take precedence over the terms of the customer

1. These terms and conditions apply to all contracts for the sale of Goods to, or provision of work for, the Customer to the exclusion of any terms and conditions specified by the Customer.

this states that the supplier does not have to stand by the price in brochures and catalogues

2. All prices quoted in brochures or catalogues are subject to confirmation at time of order and are exclusive of VAT which will be chargeable in accordance with legislation current at the date of supply.

this states that the supplier can cancel a credit limit if it wishes to

3. Credit limits may be given to approved accounts at the sole discretion of the Company but the Company will require both bank and trade references. At its sole option the Company may cancel or amend a credit limit previously granted.

this states that payments have to be made within 30 days of the invoice date

4. Payment of accounts must be effected within 30 days of Invoice date. Failure to effect payment when due will result in suspension of deliveries without prejudice to any other remedy which the Company may have.

this is the 'retention of title' clause referred to in the last chapter

5. Title in all Goods supplied by the Company shall vest in the Company until the Company has received full payment in respect thereof.

more terminology relating to contracts

There are some further terms relating to contracts which you should be aware of. When you read through these terms you will see that most of them are not likely to affect commercial contracts for the granting of credit – or at least you will hope that this will not be the case!

- **capacity** – a person (and this includes a limited company) must have the legal capacity to enter into a contract; people who do not have capacity include, for example, minors (people under 18), people of unsound mind, alien enemies and drunkards

- **consent** – a contract and any amendment to a contract requires the consent of all parties to the contract

- **void contracts** – a contract which is basically against the principles of the law, for example a contract killing

- **voidable contracts** – contracts which may be set aside because one of the parties entered into it when pressurised to do so, or when he or she was drunk or insane

- **unenforceable contracts** – a contract that is valid (ie it is not void), but the court will not enforce it – either because certain elements of the contract are missing, or even because the contract is for an immoral arrangement, eg a contract of prostitution

SELLING AND STATUTE LAW

There are a number of statutes (Acts of Parliament) which govern the way in which goods and services are sold, and these obviously affect the way in which businesses operate.

Note that a credit control department cannot exclude these statutes through clever wording of terms and conditions. They are part of English statute law and are binding on all relevant business dealings.

The principal statutes are the Trade Descriptions Act, the Sale of Goods Act (as amended), the Consumer Credit Act and the Unfair Contract Terms Act.

Trade Descriptions Act

The Trade Descriptions Act makes it a criminal offence:

■ to make false statements about goods offered for sale

■ to make misleading statements about services

Examples of offences therefore include:

■ stating that a car for sale has clocked up 15,000 miles, when in fact the figure is 25,000 miles

■ making a misleading statement about the price of goods, eg saying 'Now only £49.95, was £99.95' when it has only ever sold for £69.95

■ making a misleading statement about a service, eg 'our dry cleaning is guaranteed to remove every stain' when it does not, or 'our apartments are within easy reach of the sea' when they are fifteen miles away

Sale of Goods Act 1979

This Act and subsequent amendments (including the Supply of Goods and Services Act 1982) state that you are entitled to expect any goods that you receive from a seller to be:

of 'satisfactory quality'
This means they must meet the standard that a 'reasonable' person would expect given the description and the price.

'fit for the purpose'
The goods must do what they are supposed to do, or what the seller claims they can do: an umbrella should keep the rain out, a watch should keep accurate time.

'as described'
The goods must be what they are claimed to be: a 'leather coat' must be made of leather, a 'surround sound cinema system' must provide surround sound.

If any of these three conditions is not met, the purchaser is entitled to a full or a part refund, depending on how soon the fault appears, how serious it is and how quickly the matter is taken up. Note also the following points:

■ the purchaser can accept replacement goods, but can also insist on a refund if a replacement is not wanted

■ title to (ie ownership of) the goods passes from the seller to the purchaser when the parties to the contract (the seller and the purchaser) **intend** that it should be transferred, which is normally on the delivery of the goods; note that this could be subject to a 'retention of title' clause (see page 53)

Consumer Credit Act 1974

The Consumer Credit Act regulates the majority of **credit agreements**, eg credit and store cards, personal loans and overdrafts. Its main aim is to prevent the consumer being 'ripped off' and pressurised into signing an unsuitable credit agreement. The consumer is given a variety of 'cooling off' rights, depending on where the agreement was signed and in whose presence.

The consumer is also protected by this Act which states that the seller of goods and services between £100 and £30,000 and the credit provider have 'equal liability' for breach of contract or misrepresentation. This means that if you buy goods or book a holiday using a credit card and the seller 'goes bust' you can claim from the credit card company for loss incurred. If a business is in the retail sector, knowledge of this piece of consumer legislation is very important.

A credit agreement governs the following types of contracts:

■ **Credit sale agreements** – ie finance options for the purchase of goods and services. This is basically a loan to cover the purchase price of the item, with the loan paid back in instalments over a period of months or years. The item is owned from the date the contract is signed.

■ **Hire purchase (HP) agreements** – this is where the consumer pays monthly instalments to hire the item, but will not legally own it until the final instalment has been paid.

■ **Hire agreements** – this is the hire of goods in return for a monthly payment. The consumer will never own the item, but must keep up the payments for the term of the contract to avoid having the goods repossessed and being sued for the outstanding debt.

Unfair Contract Terms Act

Any organisation that tries to insist on **unfair terms** (eg in small print on the back of a sales contract) may be in breach of the Unfair Contract Terms Act. This would protect, for example, holidaymakers who are not put up in the hotel they booked because the small print stated that the holiday company had the right to move them to another resort. This would be seen as an 'unfair term' and would enable the holidaymaker to seek compensation. In short, a business cannot 'contract out' through the small print.

It must be stressed that the terms must be 'unfair' in order to break the law. Terms and conditions on sales documentation are normally carefully worded so that they will stand up to examination in a court of law. Generally speaking, the supplier has the upper hand in dictating terms, as you can see on the contract excerpt on page 69.

We will describe the processes of taking court action for the recovery of debt in Chapter 6.

Late Payment of Commercial Debts (Interest) Act

This Act gives a supplier an statutory right to claim interest from a customer when payment is withheld. See page 53 for a full explanation of how this works in practice. The formula for calculating the interest is:

$$\textit{Amount including VAT} \ \times \ \textit{(base rate + 8\%)} \ \times \ \frac{\textit{Number of days debt overdue}}{365}$$

Data Protection Act, 1998

When an organisation asks for a reference from a company, bank or credit reference agency, it is asking that organisation to disclose data it holds which relates to a third party (someone else). The law is very strict on this point as there is a real danger that the information may be incorrect or the person or organisation to which it relates does not want it to be released.

The current legislation covering this area is the **Data Protection Act 1998**, which applies to:

• data about **individuals** (eg sole traders, partners) but **not about companies**

• records held on computer – eg a computer database of names, addresses, telephone numbers, sales details of each customer ('data subject')

• manual records – eg a card index file system of customers details

All organisations which process personal data should register with the Data Protection Commission and should follow the eight **guiding principles** set out in the Data Protection Act. These principles require that personal data is handled properly. They state that personal data must be:

1   fairly and lawfully processed

2   processed for limited purposes

3   adequate, relevant and not excessive

4 accurate

5 not kept for longer than is necessary

6 processed in line with the data subject's rights

7 kept securely

8 not transferred to countries outside the European Union unless it is adequately protected in those countries

Individuals have the legal right to know what personal details about them are held by an organisation such as a credit reference agency. They should apply in writing to that organisation for a copy of the personal data held on file; they are likely to have to pay a small fee for this service.

Chapter Summary

■ Every time an organisation sells goods or services it enters into a contract – a legally binding agreement – with its customer. If the customer defaults on these terms, a breach of contract occurs which could be grounds for court action if the case is seen as being sufficiently serious.

■ A contract has three elements: an agreement (which involves offer and acceptance, a bargain (which involves the passing of value) and the intention to create legal relations.

■ An invitation to treat is an invitation to a person to make an offer and is not a contract.

■ A breach of contract in the case of a contract for sale of goods or services could lead to a court action for money compensation (action for price).

■ Interest on late payments is also legally enforceable under the Late Payment of Commercial Debts (Interest) Act 1998.

■ The terms and conditions of the contract of sale are often set out on the back of sales documentation and may refer back to the original credit terms communicated to the customer when the account was opened.

■ Sales of goods and services are also regulated by statute law, including the Trade Descriptions Act, the Sale of Goods Act, The Consumer Credit Act and the Unfair Contract Terms Act. An organisation is bound by all this legislation and cannot contract out of its terms.

■ A further statute which employees must take care to observe is the Data Protection Act which relates to the release of personal information, such as would be involved when a credit reference is given.

Key Terms		
	contract	a legally binding agreement enforceable in a court of law; it has three elements:
		1 an agreement, comprising an offer and an acceptance
		2 a bargain, ie value passing between the two parties (also known as 'consideration')
		3 an intention to create legal relations, ie a commercial agreement which could be taken to a court of law if the need arose
	invitation to treat	an invitation to make an offer (eg catalogue, shop window) – not a contract
	breach of contract	breaking of the terms of a contract and grounds for taking legal action
	damages	money compensation for loss or injury
	action for the price	taking legal action in the courts for recovery of an unpaid debt
	retention of title	the right of a seller of goods to retain ownership of the goods until payment is made
	Trade Descriptions Act	makes it a criminal offence for a seller to make false and misleading statements about goods and services
	Sale of Goods Act	goods sold should be of satisfactory quality, fit for the purpose and as described by the seller
	Consumer Credit Act	regulates credit agreements made by consumers, eg credit cards, personal loans and hire purchase – helps prevent pressure selling and provides cooling off periods
	Unfair Contract Terms Act	regulates against unfair terms ('small print clauses') in contracts
	Late Payment of Commercial Debts (Interest) Act 1998	allows suppliers to charge interest on overdue amounts (amended by the Late Payment of Commercial Debts Regulations 2013)
	Data Protection Act	protects confidentiality of personal data held by an organisation relating to individuals (not companies)

Activities

4.1 The features which must always be present to create a valid contract are:

(a) offer, acceptance, consideration, specific performance

(b) offer, acceptance, bargain, retention of title

(c) offer, acceptance, consideration, expiry date

(d) offer, acceptance, consideration, intention to create legal relations

Which **one** of these options is correct?

4.2 Consideration in a contract is:

(a) taking advice before entering into a contract

(b) the promise by both parties to exchange value

(c) the need for both parties to have capacity to contract

(d) the intention to create legal relations

Which **one** of these options is correct?

4.3 An offer in a contract is:

(a) the agreed bargain

(b) the agreement of a fixed price

(c) a buyer signing a purchase order

(d) the price agreed for a purchase

Which **one** of these options is correct?

4.4 Carlo shops for sugar in a supermarket. A contract is formed when:

(a) he ticks the sugar off on his shopping list

(b) he takes the sugar off the shelf and puts it in his trolley

(c) he places the sugar on the checkout conveyor belt

(d) the checkout assistant scans the sugar and the price shows on the display

Which **one** of these options is correct?

4.5 Maria agrees to do some cleaning for her friend, Carlo, as a favour. After she has done the work he promises to give her £10 because he is so pleased with it. This constitutes a valid contract.

True or False? State your reasons for your answer.

4.6 W Rooney looks at some new Nike football boots on a website and sees that one pair is advertised at £67.99 'with 30% off'. He wants to purchase them. This price is:

(a) contractually binding

(b) an invitation to treat

(c) an example of specific performance

(d) an acceptance

Which **one** of these options is correct?

4.7 K Hallett Ltd orders some goods from LFC Supplies but K Hallett Ltd fails to pay. LFC Supplies has the right under the contract to take K Hallett Ltd to court and sue for the money. This is known as:

(a) an action for the price

(b) retention of title

(c) an action for consideration

(d) an intention to create legal relations

Which **one** of these options is correct?

4.8 A written contract that may be set aside because one of the parties was pressurised into signing it is known as:

(a) a void contract

(b) a voidable contract

(c) an unenforceable contract

(d) an illegal contract

Which **one** of these options is correct?

4.9 The Sale of Goods Act states that a buyer of goods should expect the goods to be:

(a) of satisfactory quality, fit for the purpose, sold at the price stated on the price ticket

(b) of satisfactory quality, fit for the purpose, sold at the price requested at the checkout

(c) of satisfactory quality, fit for the purpose, as described

(d) of acceptable quality, fit for the purpose, as described

Which **one** of these options is correct?

4.10   The Trade Descriptions Act makes it an offence to:

(a)   sell goods that are not fit for purpose

(b)   make a false statement about the nature of your business

(c)   sell goods that are less than satisfactory in quality

(d)   make a false or misleading statement about goods offered for sale

Which **one** of these options is correct?

4.11   The Consumer Credit Act regulates the giving of credit references on customers.

True or False?

4.12   If the current bank base rate is 1%, the interest rate chargeable under the Late Payment of Commercial Debts (Interest) Act is:

(a)   10%

(b)   10.5%

(c)   9%

(d)   9.5%

Which **one** of these options is correct?

4.13   A customer owes £10,000 and the debt is 45 days late. The Bank of England base rate is 2%.

Calculate the interest charge under the Late Payment of Commercial Debts (Interest) Act to the nearest penny:

£

4.14   The Data Protection Act protects the data held by an organisation relating to:

(a)   only companies

(b)   companies and individuals

(c)   only individuals

(d)   only businesses

Which **one** of these options is correct?

5 Monitoring and controlling customer accounts

this chapter covers...

In the last three chapters we described the credit assessment of customers and the opening of sales ledger accounts. In this chapter we move to the third stage in the credit control process (shown inside the dotted line on the next page) and explain how sales ledger accounts are monitored using various analytical techniques which include:

- *the trade receivables analysis*
- *comparing customer accounts with average periods of credit*
- *the 80/20 rule*

Particular emphasis will be given to the trade receivables analysis which shows:

- *the extent to which individual accounts have debts outstanding*
- *average periods of credit given to sales ledger accounts as a whole*
- *the warning signs of accounts turning into doubtful and irrecoverable debts*

This chapter describes how debts are chased and customers are persuaded to pay on time, so helping the liquidity of the organisation. These procedures are carried out in line with an organisation's credit policy document.

This chapter also looks at alternative methods of collecting debts, including:

- *credit insurance (insuring against irrecoverable debts)*
- *factoring and invoice discounting (lending money against invoices issued)*

In the next and final chapter we pass on to the last stage in the credit control process and describe how an organisation deals with customers that will not or cannot pay invoices, either because they are short of cash, or because they are insolvent.

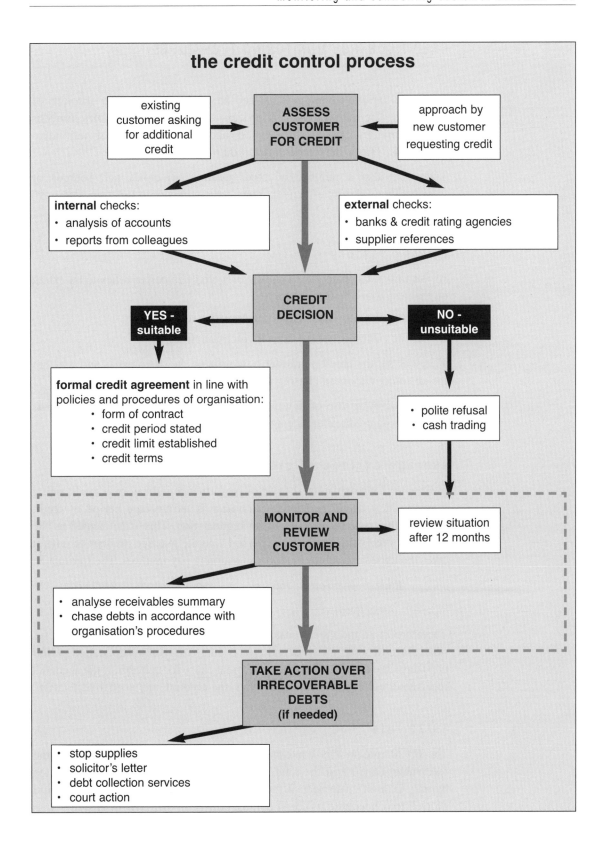

the credit control process

ASSESS CUSTOMER FOR CREDIT

existing customer asking for additional credit

approach by new customer requesting credit

internal checks:
- analysis of accounts
- reports from colleagues

external checks:
- banks & credit rating agencies
- supplier references

CREDIT DECISION

YES - suitable

NO - unsuitable

formal credit agreement in line with policies and procedures of organisation:
- form of contract
- credit period stated
- credit limit established
- credit terms

- polite refusal
- cash trading

MONITOR AND REVIEW CUSTOMER

review situation after 12 months

- analyse receivables summary
- chase debts in accordance with organisation's procedures

TAKE ACTION OVER IRRECOVERABLE DEBTS (if needed)

- stop supplies
- solicitor's letter
- debt collection services
- court action

CREDIT CONTROL MONITORING TECHNIQUES

There are various techniques that can be used to monitor the accounts of customers. The main monitoring process is the **trade receivables analysis** which provides critical information about the accounts of individual customers. This is described in detail on the pages that follow.

There are also a number of other guiding principles and sources of information used in an effectively managed credit control function. These are described below.

trading history

As we saw in Chapter 3 the analysis of a credit customer relies to an extent on the customer's trading history:

- has the customer kept within the agreed credit limit?
- has the customer settled sales invoices on time?

This will tell the credit controller how reliable the customer is and whether the customer may need chasing up.

This can also, in case of any doubt, be backed up by the taking of **status reports** from credit reference agencies.

average periods of credit

In Chapter 2 we explained the use of performance indicators in credit rating a customer. A useful benchmark indicator is the average period of credit given to the trade receivables of an organisation. This is calculated as the **accounts receivables collection period** – ie the average number of days it takes the trade receivables of an organisation to pay invoices. The formula is:

$$\frac{trade\ receivables\ \times\ 365}{sales\ revenue} = average\ length\ of\ credit\ taken$$

Therefore, if an individual customer given 30 days terms is taking 40 days on average to settle invoices and the accounts receivables collection period is 50 days, the customer may not give great cause for concern. If the accounts receivables collection period is 30 days, the account may need investigation.

80/20 rule

The 80/20 rule in this context states that 80% of the total value of the receivables (ie 80% of the total of the sales ledger balances) is represented by only 20% of customers. It therefore follows that the organisation would do well to concentrate its credit control efforts on that 20% of customers.

materiality

It follows that the remaining 80% of customers (and 20% of the sales ledger balances outstanding) are not as **material** to the credit control process as the top 20% of customers.

You may well have studied **materiality** as an accounting concept. This states that certain amounts are of such low value that they are not worth recording. If a customer, for example, has a balance due of £5 on an account, possibly because of some mix up in calculating the amount paid, this will not be **material** and is unlikely to be chased up, apart from the sending of a statement.

TRADE RECEIVABLES ANALYSIS

trade receivables analysis and liquidity

A **trade receivables analysis** is a summary of amounts owed by customers, analysed into time period columns showing how long the amounts have been outstanding. It shows the organisation the customers that are slow in settling invoices and the customers that may become irrecoverable debts.

A trade receivables analysis is an essential report which pinpoints the cause of potential **liquidity** problems and is critical in the process of liquidity management. Funds not received from trade receivables will need to be financed from elsewhere and will increase the costs of the organisation.

format of a trade receivables analysis

A trade receivables analysis can either be drawn up **manually**, or it can be printed out as a report from a **computer accounting package**. There is no 'set' format for the trade receivables analysis, but the report normally follows the same columnar pattern.

An example of a computer printed trade receivables analysis from a computer accounting package is shown and explained at the top of the next page. An alternative spreadsheet version, showing percentages of the periods for which amounts have been outstanding, is shown at the bottom of the next page.

The **credit control policy** of the organisation will normally state when the trade receivables analysis should be produced. This is normally after the end of each month after the statements have been sent out. From the analysis the organisation decides which customers it is going to chase up, and how. It may send a letter or an email, or it may telephone the customer. Again, the credit control policy will set out guidelines for how and when communications should be sent.

The illustration below shows a trade receivables analysis (also known as an 'aged debtors analysis') produced as a report from the Sales Ledger in a proprietary computer accounting program.

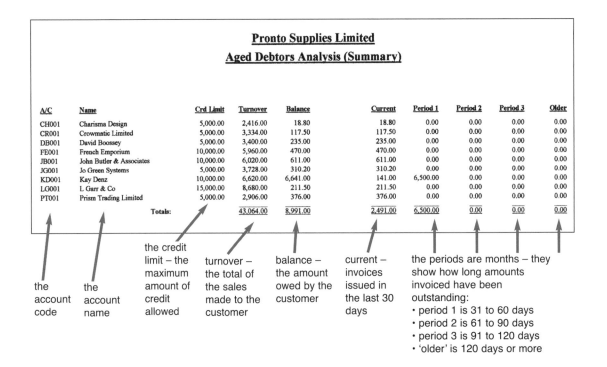

A trade receivables analysis can also be set out on a spreadsheet, as seen in the illustration below.

FAIRARM FOODS			TRADE RECEIVABLES ANALYSIS				31 July
Account	Account number	Credit Limit	Balance	up to 30 days	31 - 60 days	61 - 90 days	91 days & over
Droof & Co	8721	1000.00	164.50	164.50	0.00	0.00	0.00
Flagand Ltd	8532	750.00	376.00	376.00	0.00	0.00	0.00
Granaro Supplies	8612	750.00	499.38	499.38	0.00	0.00	0.00
Les Gola Restaurant	7951	2000.00	1632.75	799.00	833.75	0.00	0.00
Romrod Designs	6025	2000.00	1926.88	380.00	0.00	1046.88	500.00
TOTALS			4599.51	2218.88	833.75	1046.88	500.00
Percentage			100%	48%	18%	23%	11%

how to use the trade receivables analysis

The columns of the trade receivables analysis on the previous page include:

■ **account name and account number**

Note that most receivables analyses will have more accounts than are shown here – possibly hundreds, shown in alphabetical order for ease of reference. This report is shortened for the purposes of illustration.

The sales ledger account number is listed for reference purposes. In the case of the computer analysis, the account number is the computer account number allocated to the sales ledger account.

■ **credit limit and balance columns**

These two columns are compared to find out whether any customer is exceeding the allocated credit limit.

■ **invoice 'age' columns**

The remaining four columns here show how long the invoices which make up the total balance column have been outstanding.

Note that in the case of the second trade receivables analysis, the percentage outstanding for each period is shown in a row below the totals.

When analysing the report, the credit controller will look not only at individual accounts, but also at a number of relationships and trends by comparing this report with the previous month's analysis. For example, the percentages on the bottom row will indicate how quickly invoices are being settled. If percentages towards the right start to rise, there will be pressure on the company's liquidity, which will be seen in the company's bank balance.

Analysis of individual accounts is likely to start with a look at the far right-hand column. Are there any accounts with invoices which are well overdue? The £500 for Romrod Designs (second analysis), outstanding for over 91 days, could indicate a number of situations and will need to be investigated:

■ the invoice (or invoices) might be subject to a dispute and remain unpaid

■ extended credit may have been given on the invoice(s)

■ Romrod Designs may be experiencing cash flow problems

This process will then continue as each column from right to left is scrutinised for 'out-of-order' amounts. Whatever the situation, action will need to be taken, in line with the Credit Control Policy.

Are there any accounts which are exceeding their credit limit? This will be picked up from a comparison of the credit limit and balance columns for each customer. Any excess of the limit will need to be investigated and action taken according to the guidelines in the Credit Control Policy.

It is normal practice for any action taken to be written on the report, eg 'send Letter 1 . . . telephone customer . . . threaten legal proceedings' and so on.

TRADE RECEIVABLES ANALYSIS – TAKING ACTION

Credit Control Policy

Most organisations will have a Credit Control Policy which sets out the procedures for chasing debts and guidelines for the timing of:

- invoices and statements of accounts sent to the customer

- production of the trade receivables analysis

- the making of telephone calls chasing overdue invoices

- the sending of emails or faxes chasing overdue invoices

- the sending of letters chasing overdue invoices

- setting up a meeting with the customer to discuss non-payment

- placing a customer on a 'stop' list, withdrawing further credit

- sending a letter threatening legal action

- taking legal action

An example of a Credit Control Policy is shown below. Note the instructions set out in the 'Debt Collection' section.

CREDIT POLICY & PROCEDURES

New Accounts	1	One bank reference and two trade references required.
	2	Analysis of minimum of three years' accounts for limited company customers.
Credit Terms	3	Standard terms 30 days from invoice. Any extension to be authorised by Credit Controller.
	4	2.5% settlement discount at Credit Controller's discretion.
Debt Collection	5	Invoices despatched on day of issue.
	6	Statements despatched first week of the month.
	7	Trade receivables analysis produced and analysed first week of the month.
	8	Reminder letter sent first week of the month for accounts 30 days overdue (Letter 1).
	9	Telephone chaser for accounts 45 days overdue. Meeting arranged if required.
	10	Customer on stop list if no payment received within 15 days of telephone chaser (unless meeting arranged). Sales Department notified.
	11	Letter placing account on stop and threatening legal action if payment not received within seven days (Letter 2).
	12	Legal proceedings set in motion if payment not received within 30 days of Letter 2 – subject to authorisation by Finance Director and notification of Sales Manager.

standard communications

The organisation is likely to have a set of standard **letters** which will vary in tone from the polite request for payment to the formal threatening of legal action. Even if the organisation does not have a written Policy, it is likely to have standard letters in its files. It is important that the standard letters are used as they will be designed to place the organisation that issues the invoices in a strong position if legal action becomes necessary. This is covered in full in the next chapter.

The **telephone** is a very efficient means of communicating a message and assessing reasons for non-payment. A letter can easily be put in a file and ignored, but a telephone call from a persistent supplier is difficult to ignore.

The chart below shows how an invoice can be chased. It is important to note that this is only an example and not a definitive method – different organisations will have different policies and processes.

We will explain the use of letters and the telephone in chasing debt in more detail in the pages that follow.

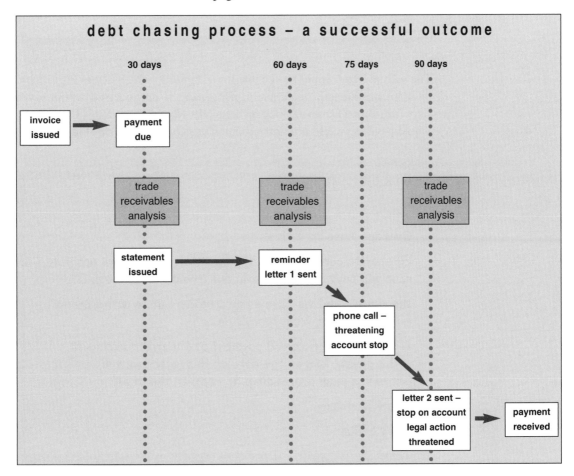

examples of letters

The first of the letter texts shown here is suitable for a 'Letter 1', ie the first chaser letter sent out (see item 8 in the Policy on page 84).

To Purchases Ledger

Dear Sir

Overdue Account 24122

We note from our records that your account balance of £10,456.50 is now overdue. The agreed payment terms are 30 days of invoice date.

Please settle this outstanding amount without delay.

We attach an up-to-date statement.

Yours faithfully

Sales Ledger

The second letter would be suitable for a 'Letter 2' which places the account on stop and threatens legal action if payment is not received within seven days (see item 11 in the Policy on page 84). Note that the Sales Department would have to be told promptly about any account placed on stop.

To Purchases Ledger

Dear Sir

Overdue Account 24122

Further to our letter of . . . . we note that we have not yet received payment of the overdue amount of £10,456.50.

We regret that we have no alternative but to withdraw our credit facilities from today's date.

If we have not received payment of the overdue amount within seven days of the date of this letter we will commence legal proceedings to recover the debt.

Yours faithfully

Sales Ledger

using the telephone

The telephone is normally resorted to when statements and letters fail to have any effect. The telephone is a useful means of communication because it demands an immediate reply.

Organisations with a poor payment record will often come up with a variety of lame and blatantly untrue excuses on the telephone. It is the job of the person chasing the debts to have ready answers for all of these. A careful note should be made of all conversations. The table below provides some common examples of excuses and possible replies.

customer excuse	your response
'We have not received the invoice.'	'We will fax/email a copy today. Please let me know for whose attention it should be marked.'
	Comment: *A very common excuse. When sending a copy, ensure that it is addressed to the right person and is accompanied by a request for immediate payment.*
'There is nobody here to authorise the payment (or sign the cheque).'	'When will the authorised person be back? Are there any pre-signed cheques in the office?'
	Comment: *Do not accept the suggestion that there is unlikely to be anyone around to authorise a payment – electronic or cheque – there should always be someone who has been given suitable authority.*
'The cheque is in the post.'	'Please can you confirm to which address it was sent, and when?'
'Electronic payment has been sent.'	Please can you confirm the bank sort code and account number to which the payment was sent?
	Comment: *These two excuses are all too common. Asking for precise bank details of the payment can often result in payment being made.*
'The computers are down and we can't access our online account.'	'Can you tell me when they are likely to be working again? Can you send us a cheque instead?'
	Comment: *This is another lame excuse, although it is more likely to be true. You should insist that if the delay is an extended one (ie days rather than hours), the customer should issue a cheque instead.*

trade receivables analysis – using discretion

It is important to appreciate that the debt-chasing actions carried out as a result of the monthly check through the trade receivables analysis should reflect the standing and payment record of each customer. Any Credit Control Policy cannot be relied upon to work 'by formula'.

For example, a **major customer** who accounts for a significant percentage of sales turnover and always pays up in the end will be treated with respect and will not necessarily be hounded for every overdue invoice. It is more likely that a diplomatic telephone call will achieve the desired result.

Conversely a relatively **small customer** with a poor payment record will be given less benefit of the doubt and will be pressed hard for overdue payments.

DOUBTFUL AND IRRECOVERABLE DEBTS

Part of the job of the person working in credit control is to assess from the information to hand if a customer is going to default and not pay the balance due. The available information might include:

■ **the trade receivables analysis** – the extent to which a customer's amounts owing are concentrated in the right-hand columns, ie to what extent they are overdue

■ **internal information provided by the sales team** – they will know from visits and meetings if the customer bears the 'tell tale' signs of struggling financially, eg selling off assets, stockpiling, reducing the price of stock

■ **internal information provided by the credit control staff** – the customer not responding to chasers, the customer providing poor excuses for non-payment, the customer's finance staff not taking telephone calls

■ **comments from other organisations in the trade**, eg 'I know that ABC Limited is struggling' or 'I hear that ABC Limited staff wages are in arrears' or 'the ABC Limited MD has sold his Porsche'

doubtful debts

If a customer looks like he/she/it is going to default, the debt is said, for obvious reasons, to be '**doubtful**'. All this means is that the organisation, weighing up the probabilities, reckons that it is unlikely that it will get paid.

There is still a possibility that the money will come in, but it is 'doubtful'.

methods of making provision for doubtful debts

As you will know from your earlier studies, organisations adjust their accounting records by making **provision for doubtful debts** and setting the provision off against profits in a 'provision for doubtful debts account'. This provision is often **a set percentage**, eg 2%, of the total trade receivables, the percentage being based on experience within that type of organisation. If this method is adopted, the day-to-day running of credit control based on the trade receivables analysis will **not** be affected by the making of the provision.

Another method of making provisions for doubtful debts is to **carry out the process for individual debts** rather than relying on a percentage of total trade receivables. This means that each time the organisation assesses the trade receivables analysis, individual accounts which look unlikely to pay up are marked up for a doubtful debt provision, referred to management (eg the Credit Controller) and entered in a 'provision for doubtful debts account'. This is a less common method, largely because it is far more involved and time-consuming, but it is a method which features in assessments which require that you 'indicate accounts for which provision should be made'. This method is featured in the Case Study which follows.

dealing with irrecoverable debts

Irrecoverable debts are doubtful debts which have lost the element of doubt – it is considered by the organisation that they will definitely not be paid and will need to be written off in the accounts against profits in an 'irrecoverable debts written off account'. The treatment of irrecoverable debts and the situations which cause them are covered in detail in the next chapter.

Case Study

RENARD LIMITED: CREDIT CONTROL PROCEDURES

situation

You work as a credit control clerk for Renard Limited, a company that manufactures and sells brushes. Normal trading terms are 30 days after invoice date.

An extract from the company's trade receivables analysis and its Credit Control Policy are set out below, together with notes on the individual customer accounts.

You are asked to write an email to Gordon White, Credit Controller, to

- analyse the situation of the four accounts in the trade receivables analysis
- recommend action that should be taken
- recommend whether any provision for doubtful debts should be made

TRADE RECEIVABLES ANALYSIS					
Customer	Total due	1 - 30 days	31 - 60 days	61 - 90 days	91 days and over
Bruin Ltd	10,200.00				10,200.00
Ottaway Trading	4,100.00	2,340.00	950.00		810.00
R C Ratz	1,500.00		500.00	1,000.00	
S Quirrel	15,570.00	9,654.00	3,560.00	2,356.00	

CREDIT CONTROL POLICY (extract)

Debt Collection

1　Invoices to be issued on day goods are despatched.

2　Statements despatched first week of the month.

3　Trade receivables analysis produced first week of each month.

4　Reminder letter sent when a debt is 30 days overdue.

5　Telephone chaser for accounts when a debt is 45 days overdue.

6　Second letter and customer on stop list when debt is 60 days overdue and a meeting arranged with customer as soon as possible.

7　Letter threatening legal action is sent when debt is 90 days overdue.

8　Legal proceedings set in motion when debt is 120 days overdue, subject to agreement of Finance Director.

CUSTOMER BACKGROUND NOTES

Bruin Limited   No orders have been received from this customer for some months. No responses have been made to chaser letters. Telephone calls have been answered by the switchboard operator but the finance staff have always been unavailable.

Ottaway Trading   This account has been trading normally, but occasionally invoices have been overlooked or lost because of inefficiency. Reminder letters have been sent and a telephone call made about the £810 invoice, when the response was 'We will look into it.'

R C Ratz   Roland Ratz has been trading with you for a number of years and generally takes 60 days rather than 30 days to pay. Invoices have never been known to be outstanding for longer than 90 days.

S Quirrel   Sam Quirrel has only been trading with you for six months. He has a new business which is expanding rapidly. Last week he asked for an increase in his limit. He has not responded to earlier chasers.

EMAIL

to Gordon White, Credit Controller

from A Student

date today

subject Credit control: problem customers

Bruin Limited

This account gives cause for concern. They have ceased trading with our company. An invoice for £10,200 remains unpaid and has been outstanding for over 90 days. Indications are that the company is in financial difficulties. We should send our letter threatening legal action and bring the matter to the attention of the Finance Director. It would be worthwhile making enquiries in the trade if anything is known of this company's financial state. It is recommended that a provision for doubtful debts should be made for this debt.

Ottaway Trading

This account has always paid eventually. A telephone chaser should be made about the £950 short-term overdue amount and a definite date for payment agreed. The £810 may either be a lost or a disputed invoice. This must also be chased on the telephone and the problem resolved promptly. No provision for doubtful debts need be made.

R C Ratz

This is a good account which has been with us for a number of years. A reminder letter should be sent about the overdue amounts (£1,500) but no further action should be taken. No provision for doubtful debts need be made.

S Quirrel

This situation gives considerable cause for concern. It is very likely that this new customer is overtrading and financing his liquidity at our expense – by not paying invoices. His request for an increased limit would confirm this. He has therefore become a substantial credit risk. Recommended actions are to place the account on stop and demand repayment of the overdue £5,916 by return. This should be set out in a formal letter. The due dates of the current invoices should be put in the diary and the amounts chased if not received on time. It is recommended that a provision for doubtful debts should be made for this debt. Sales Department should be notified of our action.

OTHER METHODS OF COLLECTING TRADE DEBTS

There are a number of financial services available to organisations which can help them with debt collection and the avoidance of irrecoverable debts. These services are provided by banks, insurance and other financial institutions. They will improve or safeguard the liquidity of the organisation, but at a cost. They include:

- **credit insurance** – insuring against the risk of non-payment, both in the UK and overseas
- **factoring** – employing a finance company to run the sales ledger and in some cases insure against irrecoverable debts
- **invoice discounting** – borrowing money against invoices

We will explain these in turn.

UK sales – credit insurance

Credit insurance replaces cash lost when a debt becomes irrecoverable. Typical options include:

- **whole turnover insurance** – general (up to 90%) coverage in the case of receivable default (non-payment of debts)
- insurance limited to **key accounts** – up to 40 customers with up to 100% coverage
- **single account** insurance – 100% cover

Overseas credit insurance is also available to cover the risk of non-payment by overseas customers either through customer default or through political events.

Credit insurance is covered in full on page 54.

factoring

A factoring company lends money against the invoices received from trade receivables of the business, providing liquidity before the invoice due dates. The factoring company takes over the administration of the sales ledger. It will normally lend up to 90% of outstanding invoice amounts as soon as the invoice is issued and will pay the balance (less charges) when the receivable settles.

Factoring companies also provide an optional irrecoverable debt protection scheme – ie insurance against irrecoverable debts – known as '**non-recourse' factoring**, for which a further charge is payable.

Factoring without irrecoverable debt protection is known as **'recourse' factoring** – ie if a debt becomes irrecoverable, recourse has to be made to the customer who will have to write off the irrecoverable debt.

invoice discounting

Here a finance house lends money against invoices issued to selected customers of the organisation, but the organisation continues to operate its own sales ledger and credit management system. As a result, the customers do not realise that the financing is being carried out.

The finance house will normally only be prepared to set up invoice discounting for an organisation which has good credit management procedures in place. The finance house will generally lend between 60% to 90% of the invoice value.

effect on liquidity management

The first of the three schemes described above – **credit insurance** – safeguards liquidity and avoids the danger of a substantial customer default, an event which could have a catastrophic effect on liquidity and profitability.

The other two schemes – **factoring** and **invoice discounting** – will improve liquidity because income from sales will be received sooner rather than later. The organisation will have a reduced working capital financing cost, but will also incur charges for the services.

The organisation will need to consider carefully the cost/benefit situation. For example, in a time of high interest rates, the early receipt of money from invoices could reduce interest costs considerably. In a time of low interest rates, the benefit might only be marginal because borrowing by way of overdraft would be relatively cheap and a viable alternative.

Chapter Summary

■ There are a number of principles that can be used to monitor and control customer accounts. These include:

- examining the customer's trading history
- using the organisation's average credit period given to customers
- applying the 80/20 rule to the sales ledger
- using the concept of materiality
- analysing the receivables summary

■ The trade receivables analysis is the report used by the credit control function to provide information about how long amounts have been outstanding on each customer account. It can also show total amounts outstanding on the sales ledger by percentage over different time periods. There are normally columns in the analysis for:
  – customer name
  – customer account number
  – credit limit
  – the balance of the account
  – different time periods for amounts outstanding

■ The trade receivables analysis is normally produced as an automatic report from a computer accounting program; it can also be produced using a computer spreadsheet.

■ Most organisations will have a Credit Control Policy which gives guidelines for the actions to be taken with customer accounts which have become overdue.

■ Letters are useful in the formal process of debt collection, although they can easily be ignored by the customer. Letters are normally standardised and graded according to the seriousness of the situation.

■ Telephone calls, when used with skill, cannot be ignored and are a persuasive means of chasing overdue amounts. The person telephoning should have replies ready for the usual excuses for non-payment.

■ The standing and payment record of each customer should also be borne in mind when chasing debts. The trade receivables analysis cannot be relied upon as the sole source of information about the customer.

■ Credit insurance is available for UK sales, either for the whole of the sales ledger, or for a group of key accounts, or for single accounts. Credit insurance for exports is also available for overseas sales.

■ Factoring companies lend against trade receivables' invoices, either with irrecoverable debt cover (non-recourse factoring) or without irrecoverable debt cover (recourse factoring). The factoring company manages the sales ledger.

■ Invoice discounting involves lending money against invoices, but the organisation keeps control of its sales ledger.

■ Credit insurance, factoring and invoice discounting can all help to improve liquidity, but the cost of these schemes must be taken into account when deciding whether to use them.

average period of credit   the average period of credit given to the customers of an organisation; this is measured in days by the trade receivables collection period formula:

$$\frac{\text{trade receivables} \ \times \ 365}{\text{sales revenue}}$$

80/20 rule   the rule that about 80% of the total value of customer accounts outstanding will be represented by about 20% of the customer accounts

materiality   the accounting concept that states that insignificant amounts should be disregarded

trade receivables analysis   a summary of amounts owed by sales ledger customers, analysed into columns, showing how long the amounts have been outstanding

credit control policy   a document drawn up by an organisation which sets out procedures for managing the sales ledger, including actions to be taken in order to chase outstanding debts, eg letters, telephone calls and legal proceedings

doubtful debt   a sales ledger debt which is unlikely to be paid – but there is still the chance that it may be paid; a provision may be made in the accounts for the debt

irrecoverable debt   a sales ledger account which is written off in the books against profit

credit insurance   an insurance policy which covers the possible loss of money through a customer defaulting on payment, ie loss through an irrecoverable debt

export credit insurance   special insurance to cover the risk of non-payment by overseas customers either through customer default or through some political event

factoring   a financial service by an external company managing the sales ledger of an organisation and lending money against the organisation's invoices

invoice factoring   a service lending money against an organisation's invoices, but allowing the organisation to continue to operate its own sales ledger and credit management

Activities

5.1 The 80/20 rule applied to credit control states that:

(a) 80% of customers are normally a good credit risk and 20% will need stricter credit control

(b) about 80% of the total value of all the customers' accounts is accounted for by about 20% of the customers

(c) an organisation should concentrate its credit control policy on 80% of the customers, the remaining 20% normally being a good credit risk

(d) if a customer account becomes an irrecoverable debt, 80% of that amount can be written off against profits

Which **one** of these options is correct?

5.2 Which of the following is a list of techniques which are likely to be used in credit control?

(a) trade receivables analysis, 80/20 rule, comparison with average payables turnover period

(b) trade receivables analysis, materiality, statement of cash flows

(c) trade receivables analysis, 80/20 rule, comparison with average receivables turnover period

(d) trade receivables analysis, 80/20 rule, statement of cash flows

Which **one** of these options is correct?

5.3 A trade receivables analysis is:

(a) a summary of customers that have been trading with a business for over 10 years

(b) a summary of small debts that have been outstanding for over 12 months and may have to be written off

(c) an analysis of supplier accounts based on the amounts outstanding and the period for which they have been outstanding

(d) an analysis of customer accounts based on the amounts outstanding and the period for which they have been outstanding

Which **one** of these options is correct?

5.4 Invoice discounting is:

(a) a loan provided by a finance company against invoices issued to customers

(b) a loan provided by a finance company to the buyer against invoices issued by a supplier

(c) the provision of settlement discount on customer invoices

(d) writing off an invoice which has become a doubtful debt

Which **one** of these options is correct?

5.5 The extract below from the trade receivables analysis of Dowzee Limited shows the total amount outstanding and the period totals.

Standard terms are payment 30 days after invoice date.

The company does not have a written Credit Control Policy.

The company does not have any standard chaser letters but instead relies on sending out statements every month and making telephone calls to slow payers.

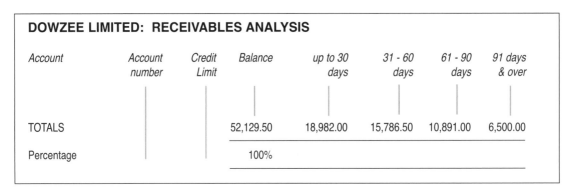

DOWZEE LIMITED: RECEIVABLES ANALYSIS

Account	Account number	Credit Limit	Balance	up to 30 days	31 - 60 days	61 - 90 days	91 days & over
TOTALS			52,129.50	18,982.00	15,786.50	10,891.00	6,500.00
Percentage			100%				

You are to:

(a) work out the percentages (to the nearest percentage) of each period total

(b) explain the effect of the situation on the liquidity of the company

(c) identify any problems with the credit control of the company

(d) suggest solutions to the problems

5.6 You are debt chasing at the beginning of the month and have a list of customers to telephone. Some of them are co-operative and agree to settle overdue amounts straightaway, but some are less helpful.

How would you deal with the following situations which all relate to amounts that are over one month overdue?

The Credit Control Policy states that a telephone chaser should be made in each case and payment by return of post requested.

(a) The customer says 'I think the cheque was posted to you yesterday, so should be with you today or tomorrow.'

(b) The customer says 'the Faster Payment electronic transfer is ready to go, but the line manager who has to sign it is off sick with a bad back.'

(c) The customer says 'Sorry, but we don't seem to have received this invoice.'

(d) The customer says 'this is in hand but our cheque issuing is now computerised and the next payment run is in ten days time in the middle of the month.'

5.7 An extract from the trade receivables analysis for S Freud Limited as at 30 November is shown below, together with details of payments received from receivables and invoices issued during November.

An extract from the Credit Control Policy of S Freud Limited is also shown below.

S Freud Limited – Trade receivables analysis as at 30 November					
Customer	Total due	1 - 30 days	31 - 60 days	61 - 90 days	91 days and over
Karl Young & Co	7,500.00				7,500.00
Fred Neesher	6,095.00	5,095.00	1,000.00		
J Bentham	499.00	100.00		399.00	

S FREUD LIMITED – CREDIT CONTROL POLICY (extract)

- One month's credit allowed from date of invoice.

- Statements despatched on first working day of the month.

- Trade receivables analysis produced at the beginning of each month.

- Reminder Letter 1 sent when account is 31 days overdue.

- Telephone chaser made when account is 45 days overdue.

- Reminder Letter 2 sent when account is 61 days overdue. This threatens legal action and account stop if payment not received within 7 days.

- Account stop and legal proceedings to be instigated and provision for doubtful debts to be made if payment not received as a result of Letter 2.

You are to:

(a) State how discussion should be conducted with any overdue accounts.

(b) Write an email dated 30 November to Ivor Pound, Credit Controller, setting out the actions which should be taken with each of the three customers (in line with the Credit Control Policy), including any recommendations for doubtful debt provision. Use your own name.

5.8 You work in the credit control section of Moore Trading Limited, a wholesaler.

You regularly review the main accounts of the business to ensure that they are trading within their limit and pay their invoices on time.

The main documents you work from are:

- the Credit Control Policy document (CCP) for Moore Trading Limited

- the monthly Trade receivables analysis

- the list of credit limits

- notes on the customer accounts compiled from the Sales Ledger section and your own previous dealings

These are all set out on the next three pages.

You are to:

(a) Review the Trade Receivables Analysis, also using the credit limit list.

(b) Review the customer account notes.

(c) Draft action points on each of the ten main accounts. These should be suitable for an email to be sent to the Credit Controller.

The plan should, for each case

- identify the customer

- analyse the current position

- suggest a course of action (if required) including any doubtful debt provision or irrecoverable debt write-off that may be necessary

CREDIT CONTROL POLICY FOR MOORE TRADING LIMITED

Current credit control procedures following the agreement of a credit limit:

1. An order for goods is received by email, fax or phone (all phone calls are recorded).

2. Goods are delivered and a goods received note is signed by the customer.

3. The goods received notes are kept in a file in the accounts office.

4. An invoice will be issued a few days after delivery on 30 day terms.

5. An analysis of trade receivables is produced monthly.

6. A reminder telephone call is made when the debt is 14 days overdue.

7. When a debt is 30 days overdue a standard chaser letter is sent.

8. When the account is 60 days overdue the account will be put on stop.

9. If the debt is 90 days overdue, it will either be placed in the hands of a debt collection company or legal proceedings may be instigated if the customer does not respond to calls or letters. The debt will be classified as a doubtful debt.

10. If the customer becomes insolvent (bankruptcy, administration, liquidation) the account should be stopped (if not already stopped) and the amount of the debt fixed and classified as a doubtful debt. Investigations should be made about any goods supplied as the title may remain with Moore Trading Limited. This is in accordance with the standard retention of title clause in the Moore Trading Limited terms and conditions issued to all customers.

MOORE TRADING LIMITED: TRADE RECEIVABLES ANALYSIS AS AT 31 MARCH					
	Balance £	**0 – 30 days** £	**31 – 60 days** £	**61 – 90 days** £	**Over 90 days** £
Customer					
Al Binoni Ltd	20,000	20,000			
B Rahms & Co	55,000				55,000
CIM Arosa Ltd	65,000	30,000	35,000		
H Umell	60,000	60,000			
L Garr Ltd	65,000		20,000	20,000	25,000
Mendell & Son	(20,000)	(20,000)			
G Reeg	45,000				45,000
B Britten Ltd	40,000	20,000	20,000		
E Whittaker Ltd	90,000	30,000	30,000	30,000	
V Williams & Co	30,000	20,000	10,000		

Customer Credit Limits	
	£
Al Binoni Ltd	40,000
B Rahms & Co	50,000
CIM Arosa Ltd	60,000
H Umell	90,000
L Garr Ltd	40,000
Mendell & Son	45,000
G Reeg	20,000
B Britten Ltd	40,000
E Whittaker Ltd	75,000
V Williams & Co	40,000

Notes on the ten main customers of Moore Trading Limited

1.   Al Binoni Ltd, a new customer with a limit of £40,000 placed its first order a few weeks ago. A new order for £15,000 of goods has just been received.

2.   B Rahms & Co have not responded to any chaser letters or telephone calls. The credit limit is £50,000.

3.   CIM Arosa Ltd is a new customer and was given a credit limit of £60,000. There was a report in the local paper that the company has had to make 20% of its staff redundant. CIM Arosa Ltd has just placed an order for another £10,000 of goods.

4.   H Umell is a long standing customer and has always settled the account within trading terms.

5.   L Garr Ltd has gone into administration. The account is not credit insured.

6.   The account of Mendell & Son is in credit because they have duplicated a payment.

7.   G Reeg is not responding to any communications.

8.   B Britten Ltd is a new business with a limit of £40,000. The company has just placed an order for £30,000 of goods but no payment has yet been made on the account.

9.   E Whittaker Ltd is a long established customer and has always paid eventually, but has a history of late payment. Moore Trading's Limited's Managing Director recently agreed to extend the terms of the account to 60 days. The account limit is £75,000.

10.   V Williams & Co has been purchasing £20,000 or less per month. The limit is £40,000.

6 Collecting debts and dealing with insolvency

this chapter covers...

In the last chapter we described the credit control process in action and explained the use of the trade receivables summary and other internal records as the basis for taking action to recover money owing from receivables.

In this chapter we take the process a stage further and describe how organisations attempt to recover amounts which the customer either will not or cannot repay. This involves a number of stages and options:

- *ensuring that there is a valid debt and underlying contract on which to base any action*
- *using debt collection agencies to recover the debt*
- *using a solicitor to recover the debt*
- *taking the customer to court to recover the debt on the basis of the contract of sale*
- *taking the customer through the insolvency courts and dealing with customers who are already insolvent*

Publisher's note: accounting and legal terminology

Please note that current **legal terminology** uses the term '**debtor**' for a person who owes money and the term '**creditor**' for a person who is owed money. The terms 'debtor' and 'creditor' are used from time-to-time in this chapter, but in the strictly legal sense.

IRRECOVERABLE DEBTS – THE FINAL FRONTIER

doubtful and irrecoverable debts

In the last chapter we saw that a **doubtful debt** is a debt that is **unlikely** to be paid and will have to be provided for in the accounts. An **irrecoverable debt**, on the other hand, is a debt that will **definitely not** be paid and will have to be written off in the accounts to the statement of profit or loss as an expense to the business.

is it worth it?

An irrecoverable debt is the final stage in the credit control process. It occurs when the organisation gives up trying to recover the debt and decides to minimise its losses by writing it off through the statement of profit or loss.

As we will see in this chapter, as the debt recovery process moves to the stage where debt collection agencies, solicitors or court action are involved, the costs start to mount up. The question has to be asked 'is it worth it?' This can happen when:

■ the debt is relatively small when compared with the cost of recovery

■ the customer looks like becoming insolvent (unable to pay debts)

■ the customer is insolvent (a bankrupt individual or company in liquidation)

It must be remembered that an organisation is only likely to recover a debt – even through court action – if the customer has the money or other realisable assets to enable the debt to be repaid. If you are working in credit control you may have to recommend irrecoverable debts for writing off. The Credit Control Policy may allow you to write off small debts (say up to £100), but you will need to refer larger amounts to the Credit Controller.

is there a contract of sale?

A **contract** is the legal agreement which should support all sales transactions. This does not mean that there has to be a formal written document relating to every invoice – a contract can be oral (word of mouth), but there does have to be an agreement which involves:

■ an offer for sale and an acceptance of the offer, eg when an order is placed by a customer

■ value changing hands both ways (eg money and goods at an agreed price)

■ the realisation by seller and buyer that the agreement has legal consequences and could end up in court if the agreement is broken

Please see Chapter 4 (pages 68-69) for details of commercial contracts.

The important point here is that if a debt is to be pursued through legal channels including solicitors and the courts, there must be a valid contract relating to it.

If the customer can show that there is no contract, the organisation has no hope of being able to recover the money. The following are examples of 'no hope' situations:

- the customer has not signed an order form where the order form is the agreement to purchase
- the goods or services have been supplied, but have not been ordered
- an order has been cancelled by the customer by email before goods were despatched

breach of contract

Legal action can be taken against a customer when a contract is in existence because non-payment is a **breach of contract** – the customer is not carrying out an agreed part of the bargain.

There are a number of **remedies** available for breach of contract in a wide variety of situations. The remedy chosen will depend on the type of contract. For example, a builder who is contracted to build a house and disappears off site before putting the roof on, can be ordered by the court to complete the work (the remedy of **specific performance**). If, however, the person having the house built refuses the builder access to the site, the builder could **terminate** the contract and demand payment for what had been done (the remedy of **quantum meruit**, which means 'what it deserves').

These situations do not have much in common with credit control in an organisation. Here the remedy of **action for the price** – ie taking legal action in the courts for recovery of an unpaid debt – is the normal remedy for breach of contract.

USING THIRD PARTIES FOR COLLECTING DEBT

When an organisation finds that its own credit control process is proving unsuccessful in getting customers to pay up, it can employ third parties, such as **debt collection agencies** and **solicitors**, to try and recover debts.

debt collection agencies

Debt collection agencies are commercial organisations that collect debts on behalf of clients. They are normally paid by taking a percentage of the amount collected. In other words, the more successful they are, the more they receive – which is a major incentive for being successful. They tend to be effective at debt collecting because after a while customers tend to ignore the credit control letters and telephone calls of the supplier, but when an independent body is called in to collect debt, they take more notice and are more likely to pay. Debt collection agencies have a distinct psychological advantage.

A typical debt collection schedule follows a number of steps in quick succession until payment is received:

Day 1	Send a chaser letter to the customer.
Day 4	Telephone the customer.
Day 12	Telephone the customer again.
Day 20	Send a letter threatening legal action.
Day 28	Start legal proceedings – suing for the debt in the courts.

Debt collection agencies can achieve a success rate of around 70%. The organisations that employ them should carefully monitor their success rates to ensure that they are operating efficiently.

solicitors

Customers do not like receiving letters from solicitors chasing debts and threatening legal action in the courts. A solicitor's letter is therefore often an effective way of recovering a well-overdue invoice.

When employing a solicitor for this purpose it is important to use a firm that specialises in debt collection. Solicitors are not cheap, nor will the Small Claims Track System (see next page) reimburse solicitors' costs, so they should only be used when there is a reasonable chance of the customer being able to repay the debt. It is also important to be precise when providing the solicitor with details of the debt and customer, eg the exact amount owed, the name and address of the customer. Any mistake might invalidate the claim.

TAKING THE CUSTOMER TO COURT

insolvency practitioners

In order to take advice about getting money back from a customer who may be insolvent, or taking a customer to court, the person or business owed the money (the 'creditor') will need to hire a **licensed insolvency practitioner**, normally from the accountancy profession. An insolvency practitioner will provide advice and if necessary represent the creditor in court.

taking court action

There are two ways in which a 'debtor' (customer) may be taken to court:

■ to **enforce repayment of the debt** – assuming that the customer is solvent and can repay debts when they are due; this is the most common form of court action taken as part of the credit control process

■ to bring about the **bankruptcy** (of an individual) or **liquidation** (of a limited company) – assuming that the debtor (customer) is insolvent and is unable to repay debts when they are due and hoping that some money will be realised from the customer's assets; this is a last resort action

We will look first at the process of taking the customer to court to enforce payment of the debt.

the court system – amounts of civil claims

The County Court deals with claims ('civil' claims) by people owed money and offers three 'tracks' for pursuing claims of differing amounts:

■ **Small Claims Track** if the claim for recovery of debt is £10,000 or less; you do not have to use a solicitor or barrister – you can present the case yourself – (this track is popularly known as the 'Small Claims Court')

■ **Fast Track** applies to the more serious cases, for claims between £10,000 and £25,000, which will normally only take one day in court to resolve

■ **Multi-Track** is for cases which will take more than one day to resolve, eg claims over £25,000 or complex cases under £25,000

When completing the paperwork for the claim to the court it is vital that details such as identifying the customer (debtor) and the debt are correct, eg:

■ the name of the individual or the company

■ the address of the individual or the company

■ the amount owing

■ the date of the debt

When the paperwork has been lodged, the court will issue a 'default summons' to the customer who can either agree to the claim (which is unlikely), ignore it (in which case judgement will go against the customer) or go ahead with the court proceedings.

the court system – what happens if you win

If the court decision goes in favour of the person or business owed the money, a County Court Judgement will be issued against the customer. The customer will either pay up, in which case the debt is repaid and all is well, or the customer will refuse to pay, either because he/she does not want to, or because he/she does not have sufficient assets to repay the debt.

One initial option to persuade the customer to pay up is a court order for an **oral examination**. The customer is required to come to court to be questioned on details of income, capital and savings. This procedure is likely to put pressure on the cross-examined customer to pay the money due.

enforcement of the judgement

If the customer does not pay up it will be necessary to apply to the court for enforcement of the judgement so that the debt can be repaid in full, or (more likely) in part. There are a number of options open to the 'creditor' (person owed the money) who wishes to enforce judgement by court order:

garnishee order	This is a court order which will be sent to a third party, eg a bank or building society which has an account for the customer, requiring the money to be paid direct to the creditor. The order will claim the due amount from the bank or building society account of the customer on that day. This will only work if the money is in the account on that day. If the account is low in funds or overdrawn, the creditor will get little or nothing. It is all a question of timing and knowing when money has been paid in, which could be difficult.
warrant of execution	This order is a request for the court bailiffs to enter the customer's home or business premises to seize belongings or assets to sell and pay off the debt. The restrictions here are that the bailiffs are not allowed to break down the door or to seize essential living items or 'tools of the trade'.
warrant of delivery	If the customer has goods which belong to the creditor (for example goods sold and covered by a 'retention of title' clause), the payable can obtain a court order – a 'warrant of delivery' – which will give the court bailiffs authority to obtain and collect the goods.
attachment of earnings	If the customer is working and earning, an Attachment of Earnings Order may be granted by the court. This will require the customer's employer to deduct a certain amount from the customer's salary on a regular basis until the debt is repaid. The judge will decide on the proportion which can be deducted, as the customer will need money for living expenses.

charging order　　If the customer owns property the creditor can apply to the court to 'register a charge' on the property to show that the creditor has an interest in the money received from the eventual sale of the property. This is more of a 'last ditch' defence and can run into major problems if the customer has family and children who will be made homeless if the property is sold.

Of these court orders, the warrant of execution (sending in the bailiffs) and attachment of earnings (deduction from salary) are the most reliable and most common remedies. If all else fails, the payable can use an insolvency practitioner and resort to the insolvency courts to bring about the sale of the customer's assets and the distribution of the money realised to **all** of the payables (creditors). This is described in detail on the next page.

'no hope' debt and 'irrecoverable' debt?

It is important to repeat at this point that it is only worth a business taking a customer to court and enforcing a court order if the customer has funds and other assets available to repay the debt. More often than not an overdue debt will be the result of a customer running into serious financial difficulties, in which case no amount of costly court action will produce any results.

The solution in this case is to write the amount off as an irrecoverable debt in the payable's accounts, where the amount can be set off through the statement of profit or loss against the tax liability of the organisation.

It is also possible to write off any VAT due on the debt through **irrecoverable debt relief** given by HMRC and reclaimable through the VAT Return.

We look further at this type of situation in the Case Study on page 113.

Retention of Title (ROT) and debt recovery

The Sale of Goods Act 1979 states that title to goods sold passes when the seller and buyer **intend** that it should. This would normally be on delivery, but by implication the law allows sellers to retain title to the goods until payment is made when this is stated in the Terms and Condition of Sale or contract as a 'Retention of Title' (ROT) clause (see page 53 for an example).

In short, the seller that has included a Retention of Title clause in the sales documentation can reclaim the goods from the buyer if the buyer will not or cannot pay, but only if:

- the goods can be clearly identified (eg by the seller's stamp or sticker)
- the goods have not been processed, improved or mixed in a manufacturing process, eg paper processed into a book

CUSTOMERS AND INSOLVENCY

the insolvency process in a nutshell

insolvency is being unable to pay debts as they fall due

A payable – the **'creditor'** – such as a trading business can take a receivable to court to prove that the trade receivable – the **'debtor'** – is insolvent. The result of this is that the court will then arrange for the debtor's assets to be sold off and **all** the payables repaid as far as is possible with the money realised by the sale. It is unlikely that the creditors will get all their money back – trade (unsecured) payables are often at the back of the queue for repayment and may receive little or nothing.

some legal terminology

The laws that cover insolvency and all its complexities are:

■ **Insolvency Act 1986**, which has been amended to some extent by further legislation, including:

■ **Enterprise Act 2002**

Further information can be found at the very helpful official website www.insolvency.gov.uk

The law is never straightforward and so there are some terms to remember:

■ an **individual** (eg sole trader or partner in a partnership) who is proved by the court to be insolvent becomes a **bankrupt**; the individual normally remains a bankrupt for 12 months, after which he/she is discharged, although arrangements to repay debt from earnings may run for a further period

■ a **limited company** that is proved by the court to be insolvent is said to be **in liquidation** – a limited company cannot therefore be said to be 'bankrupt'

the stages of the insolvency process

Suppose a business finds that a customer – a sole trader – will not pay up. The business wishes to make the customer bankrupt. The business should:

1   Ensure the debt is £750 or more (a lower amount is not sufficient for the bankruptcy process).

2   Make a 'statutory demand' to the 'debtor' (the customer) on an official form for the amount owing.

3   If payment is not received within three weeks, send in a 'creditors' petition' to the court. A meeting of all creditors (payables) may be

called by the court. Payables will be asked to send in a statement ('proof') of what they are owed by the receivable.

4   The court makes a bankruptcy order against the customer (the 'debtor') and appoints an official (the 'trustee in bankruptcy') who arranges the sale of the customer's assets (except domestic items and tools of the trade) and distributes the money to the payables in the following order of priority:

– the costs of the bankruptcy proceedings (ie court costs and fees)

– preferential debts (items such as employee wages)

– any floating charge holder (eg a bank which has a secured overdraft)

– unsecured payables such as trade payables (ie you)

You will see from this that trade suppliers of a bankrupt individual are last in the list to be paid off. What little remains after court costs, employee wages and the secured bank overdraft have been paid off in full, has then to be shared proportionally between trade suppliers. So if, for example, trade suppliers are owed £50,000 and there is only £5,000 left, they will get a 'dividend' of only 10p in the £.

Note also the following:

■ Trade suppliers who do not start the insolvency process themselves will be advised by the court when bankruptcy proceedings are under way and will be asked to send in a statement of what they are owed; they will be kept informed of the progress of the proceedings and will receive any 'dividend' in due course.

■ The process for putting limited companies into liquidation follows very much the same pattern, except that the shareholders of the company will be the last in the queue for repayment of their investment from the proceeds of the sale of assets.

administration and administrative receivers

The law is not always helpful in its choice of terminology. The terms **'administration'** and **'administrative receiver'** are a case in point. They both relate to areas of insolvency where the interests of trade suppliers are not looked after particularly well, but they relate to very different situations.

1 **Administration** is a state of affairs where an organisation which is running into solvency problems has an **administrator** appointed by the court to run its affairs. When an organisation is in administration, no other payable can petition for bankruptcy or liquidation. The organisation is protected from creditors (payables), including the bank.

2 The other situation involves a bank which has the security of a **floating charge** over the assets of a company to secure its overdraft. The security document enables the bank to appoint an **administrative receiver** to sell the secured assets of the company. In this situation the unsecured payables will again be practically last in the queue for repayment while the bank will be able to maximise the amount it receives.

In the Case Study that follows we look at a variety of situations which involve recommendations and decisions which have to be made within the Credit Control function relating to:

- debt collection

- court action

- insolvencies

- provision for doubtful debts and irrecoverable debt write offs

Case Study

WESSEX LIMITED: DEALING WITH PROBLEM ACCOUNTS

situation

You work as a credit control clerk for Wessex Limited, a company that manufactures high quality garden furniture.

At the end of the month you are asked to deal with the receivables analysis and sort out any queries relating to problem sales ledger accounts.

The main queries you have been presented with are set out below. You have been asked to:

- state what action you would take in each case

- suggest where provision for doubtful debts is to be made

- indicate if any debt is to be written off as an irrecoverable debt

You are to set out your recommendations in an email to the Credit Controller, Tom Hardy.

1 Slow paying accounts

You note from the recent receivables analysis that five accounts are more than 90 days overdue (standard terms are payment at the end of the month following the invoice date). None of the accounts is responding to your letters and telephone calls. All of the accounts have just been sent a letter threatening legal action.

Tom Hardy, the Credit Controller, has commented to you 'There's no point taking these accounts to court – we do a lot of business with them and they are probably basically sound. They just need a lot of pressure to make them pay up, a letter from a debt collection agency, for example.'

2   Wildeve Limited – disputed transaction

Wildeve Limited has a history of being an awkward customer. There is currently £1,200 more than 90 days outstanding. Your investigations show that this amount relates to a shipment of chairs which Wildeve Limited claims was not ordered. You look through your copy sales invoice file and cannot trace a purchase order or any record of how the order was placed. The latest email from the customer says "You can come and collect the goods if you wish. They are still in their original packing. You will be liable for the carriage costs."

Tom Hardy asks "Shall we call in our solicitor?"

3   John Newson – County Court debtor

You have successfully obtained a County Court judgement against John Newson for non-payment of a debt for £6,000. John Newson is a salaried purchasing manager for a chain of garden centres and has also been running a sole trader business as a landscape designer 'on the side'. You believe he has substantial assets, but he is refusing to pay, even after the court judgement.

Tom Hardy asks "What can we do to get this man to pay?"

Suggest two suitable methods of enforcing the judgement.

4   Ken Everdene – bankruptcy order

Tom Hardy brings you an official letter which is notification of a bankruptcy order made against your customer Ken Everdene. You check the account balance and your receivables analysis and find that Ken owes a total of £4,500 represented by invoices spread over a 30 to 90 day period.

5   Stourminster Consultancy Limited – notice of Administration

You have been worried about the account of Stourminster Consultancy Limited which has been overdue to the extent of £1,750 for a couple of months. You have heard from local reports that the business has been having problems in meeting its commitments. You now receive notice that it has been placed in Administration.

solution

Please see the email on the next page.

EMAIL

to   Tom Hardy, Credit Controller

from   A Student

date   today

subject Credit control: problem accounts

1   **Slow paying accounts**
    I recommend the employment of a debt collection agency. The accounts are likely to be stirred into action and make payment when the pattern of debt chasing changes and accelerates. It would be too costly and inappropriate to employ a solicitor at this stage when there is a reasonable likelihood of the money being paid. No provision for doubtful debts needs to be made yet.

2   **Wildeve Limited – disputed transaction**
    Unfortunately in this case there is no evidence of an order, which is the acceptance of our offer for sale, and so there is no valid contract. Unless evidence can be found, we will be liable for collection of the goods and will have to cancel the invoice. We cannot sue where there is no contract.

3   **John Newson – County Court debtor**
    Enforcement of the court judgement could be made either as an attachment of earnings (the receivable has a salary from his employer) or as a warrant of execution (sending the bailiffs in). Other remedies such as garnishee order, warrant of delivery or charging order will not be so effective. Provision for doubtful debts needs to be made at this stage.

4   **Ken Everdene – bankruptcy order**
    The bankruptcy order indicates that bankruptcy proceedings have commenced against this customer. We will have to complete a proof of debt form for the court, listing the invoices totalling £4,500. It is doubtful if we will receive much of a dividend, but provision for doubtful debts needs to be made at this stage. This may well become an irrecoverable debt at a later stage.

5   **Stourminster Consultancy Limited – notice of Administration**
    The fact that this company has been placed in Administration means that payables such as ourselves can do very little apart from carry out our usual debt chasing procedures. We are unable to take any legal action or consider insolvency proceedings. It would be wise to make provision for doubtful debts at this stage.

A Student

■ The credit control function of an organisation may decide to use a third party such as a debt collection agency or a solicitor to chase up debts. These third parties can often exert more pressure on a customer than the supplier.

■ The credit control process of an organisation must assess whether the process of debt collection through legal action can be justified in terms of the size of the debt and the likelihood of recovering the debt.

■ It is important that a valid contract underlies all sales transactions. If legal action is to be taken to recover a debt there must be a contract on which to sue the receivable.

■ An organisation can take a receivable to court either to enforce repayment of debt or to bring about the bankruptcy of an individual or the liquidation of a company.

■ A County Court judgement requiring the receivable to repay the debt owing is the most common outcome of legal action taken by the credit control function of an organisation.

■ If the receivable does not repay the debt after judgement has been made in the payable's favour, the payable can obtain a court order to enforce repayment. The most common of these are warrant of execution (using bailiffs to seize assets) and attachment of earnings (deduction from salary).

■ Taking court action to bring about the bankruptcy or liquidation of a receivable is another way of obtaining repayment of some element of the debt outstanding.

■ Bringing about the bankruptcy or liquidation of a receivable in the courts will result in all the assets of the receivable being sold off and distributed (in principle) to all the payables.

■ The distribution of the sale proceeds of the assets in a bankruptcy or liquidation of a receivable is made in a strict order of priority: court costs and fees, preferential payables, floating charge holders and then unsecured trade payables. Payables who are owed money on invoices are therefore last in the list and may receive little or no money.

■ The credit control function of an organisation must know about the effect of alternatives to the normal insolvency route – for example administrations and the appointment by secured payables (such as a bank) of administrative receivers. These alternatives significantly weaken the position of a trade payable.

Key Terms	**doubtful debt**	a sales ledger debt which is unlikely to be paid
	irrecoverable debt	a sales ledger account which will not be paid and is written off in the books against profit
	irrecoverable debt relief	VAT reclaimable from HMRC on a written-off debt
	contract	an agreement between two parties which must involve an offer and acceptance, the passing of value by both parties and the intention that it can form the basis of legal action if the need arises
	breach of contract	breaking of a term (or terms) of the contract which can be remedied through taking legal action in the courts
	receivable/debtor	the individual or organisation who owes the money – against whom court action may be taken
	payable/creditor	the individual or organisation who is owed the money – and who takes court action
	action for the price	taking legal action in the courts for the recovery of an unpaid debt
	debt collection agency	a commercial organisation which collects debts for third parties
	insolvency practitioner	a licensed person taken on to advise and represent a creditor in court
	Small Claims Track	the court system for pursuing civil claims of £10,000 or less
	Fast Track	the court system for pursuing civil claims of between £10,000 and £25,000 which will normally take only one day to resolve
	Multi-Track	the court system for pursuing civil claims which will take more than one day to resolve – normally those over £25,000 or complex cases under £25,000
	oral examination	a court order requiring the receivable to be cross examined in court to provide details of assets – used when the receivable refuses to pay up
	garnishee order	a court order claiming money from a third party (eg a bank account) which is owed to the payable

warrant of execution	a court order authorising the bailiffs to seize the assets of a receivable who refuses to pay up
warrant of delivery	a court order authorising the bailiffs to seize assets belonging to the payable but held by the receivable
attachment of earnings	a court order requiring an employer to deduct a proportion of the receivable's earnings and pay it to the payable
charging order	registration of a charge (interest) in a property belonging to the receivable which entitles the payable to be paid part of the money received for the property when it is sold
insolvency	being unable to pay debts as they fall due
bankruptcy	the situation where an individual (eg sole trader or partner) is taken to court and proved to be insolvent so that his/her assets can be sold and distributed to payables
liquidation	the situation where a limited company is taken to court and proved to be insolvent so that its assets can be sold and distributed to payables
statutory demand	a formal written demand to the receivable from the payable demanding repayment of a debt (at least £750) within 21 days; a necessary condition for the bankruptcy/liquidation process
trade creditors/payables	commercial organisations that supply goods and services on credit and on an unsecured basis – often the last to be paid off in insolvency proceedings
preferential creditors	payables such as employees who are owed wages by the receivable and who will be paid off in priority to trade payables
administrative receiver	an individual appointed under a floating charge (bank security) to sell the assets of the receivable when the security is called in; this ensures that the bank will be paid in priority to the trade payables
administration	where a receivable running into solvency problems has an administrator appointed by the court to run its affairs; while an administrator is in place no payable can take legal action to recover debts

Activities

6.1 A customer could refuse payment of an invoice for goods supplied by claiming that there is no valid contract when:

(a) the supplier has not offered settlement discount terms on the sales invoice as the supplier normally does

(b) the customer has not signed the purchase order which has been issued in the first place

(c) the supplier has dropped the price of the goods supplied following the placing of the order

(d) an administration order has been placed on the supplier

Which **one** of these options is correct?

6.2 When a customer is in breach of contract for non-payment the supplier will normally pursue the following remedy:

(a) an action for the price

(b) an action for specific performance

(c) an action for 'quantum meruit'

(d) an action for termination of the contract

Which **one** of these options is correct?

6.3 When a supplier wishes to claim in the courts for a customer debt of £2,500, the route he/she should take would be:

(a) the High Court

(b) the Multi-track system

(c) the Fast Track system

(d) the Small Claims Track

Which **one** of these options is correct?

6.4 An enforcement of a court judgement on a customer which involves the allocation and payment to the supplier of money on the bank account of the customer is known as a:

(a) warrant of execution

(b) warrant of delivery

(c) garnishee order

(d) charging order

Which **one** of these options is correct?

6.5 A supplier that wishes to place a statutory demand to instigate the bankruptcy process on a customer must submit a claim for an amount owing that is at least:

(a) £500

(b) £750

(c) £1,500

(d) £5,000

Which **one** of these options is correct?

6.6 You work in a credit control department and receive notice that your customer Furbo Limited, who owes £5,000, has been placed in administration.

You should:

(a) pursue the debt in the normal way

(b) petition for the company's bankruptcy

(c) obtain a warrant of delivery

(d) obtain a warrant of execution

Which **one** of these options is correct?

6.7 A Retention of Title clause will only be operative for goods supplied if the goods are

(a) used in a manufacturing process

(b) already paid for by the buyer

(c) can be clearly identified

(d) are mixed with other goods

Which **one** of these options is correct?

6.8 An Administrative Receiver is appointed to sell the assets of an company by:

(a) an insolvency order over the assets

(b) a bank with a floating charge

(c) an execution warrant

(d) an administration order

Which **one** of these options is correct?

6.9 You work for Bishop Imports which is owed £5,000 by Dodge E Trading Limited.

Dodge E Trading Limited has recently been put into liquidation.

You receive a schedule from the court stating that £400,000 has been realised by the sale of the company's assets.

The creditors (payables) that are paid out of this sum are:

- liquidation costs of £85,000
- preferential payables of £127,000 (employee wages)
- Midwest Bank floating charge to cover the company's overdraft £150,000
- Unsecured trade payables of £190,000 (including the £5,000 owed to Bishop Imports)

(a) The dividend per £1 owed that should be paid to Bishop Imports is therefore:

    (a)   76p

    (b)   100p

    (c)   80p

    (d)   20p

Which **one** of these options is correct?

(b) The amount that will be received by Bishop Imports is £.......................................

Answers to activities

CHAPTER 1: INTRODUCTION TO CREDIT CONTROL

1.1   (b)

1.2   (a)

1.3   (c)

1.4   (b)

1.5   (b)

1.6

Reference received	Risk rating			Significant word
	high	**medium**	**low**	
Centro Bank Limited		✔		should
B Ruckner Ltd		✔		normally
V Williams & Co		✔		usually

1.7   **(a)**

	True	False
You will be happy to provide the credit facilities straightaway because the company is already trading with you on a cash basis		✔
You will only need to obtain one trade reference		✔
You will need a bank reference and two trade references	✔	

(b)   (c)

1.8   (a)

CHAPTER 2: FINANCIAL ANALYSIS OF CUSTOMER ACCOUNTS

2.1 **(a)**

	Year 1	Year 2	Year 3
Current ratio	1.06	1.07	1.03
Liquid capital (quick) ratio	0.47	0.40	0.26
Accounts receivable collection period	43	43	48
Accounts payable payment period	60	63	65
Profit for the period %	2.67%	1.92%	1.94%
Interest cover	1.33	1.21	1.18
Gearing	65.8%	64.2%	67.8%

(b) Comments on performance indicators:

Liquidity

The *current* and *quick* ratios are low and give cause for concern about the ability of the company to be able to settle its liabilities on time.

The *Accounts receivable collection period* shows that customers are taking an increasingly long time to settle and provide the much needed cash, although the period of 43 to 48 days is not unusual.

The *Accounts payable payment period* shows that the company is taking increasingly long credit, which would make any new supplier cautious.

Profitability

Profit for the period % is running at a very low level and gives no confidence in the company's continuing ability to generate cash.

Interest cover shows that operating profit is barely covering interest payments. Any increase in borrowing or in interest rates could make the company's liquidity vulnerable.

Financial position

Gearing is high and has increased in Year 3, indicating a substantial reliance on borrowing.

(c) No.

2.2
    (c) An increasing number of irrecoverable debts

    (d) Suppliers not being paid on time

    (f) A decline in operating profit

    (i) An increase in level of the bank overdraft

    (j) An increasing tendency for the bank account to remain overdrawn

    (k) A substantial increase in the level of sales and no injection of capital

2.3 (a) to (c)

Customer: De Gass Limited	Indicator	Score
Operating profit margin %	16.5%	10
Interest cover	7.86	10
Current ratio	1.5	0
Gearing %	24%	20
Total score		40

Customer: Vangov Limited	Indicator	Score
Operating profit margin %	4.8%	0
Interest cover	2.28	0
Current ratio	1.27	0
Gearing %	60.4%	0
Total score		0

(d)   The level of credit risk of De Gass Limited is very low and that of Vangov Limited is medium.

(e)   De Gass Limited can be considered good for a limit of £50,000.

(f)   The accounts of Vangov Limited indicate a number of weaknesses:

- Profitability is low, with operating profit at only 4.8%, covering interest only 2.28 times.
- Liquidity is also vulnerable, with the current ratio at 1.27. Also, inventory is high at £2m, and if taken out of current assets, gives a liquid capital ratio of only 0.29 which shows that the company may have difficulty in meeting its current liabilities.
- Financial position is also questionable with gearing high at 60.4%.

CHAPTER 3: GRANTING CREDIT AND SETTING UP CUSTOMER ACCOUNTS

3.1 (d)

3.2 (b)

3.3 (a)

3.4 (c)

3.5 (b)

3.6 (a)

3.7 (c)

3.8 **(a)** 27 May **(b)** 30 June **(c)** 2 June

3.9 **(a)** 18.53%

(b) (1) No. The figure is higher than the cost of borrowing and therefore unattractive.

(2) Yes. The figure is lower than the cost of borrowing and therefore attractive.

3.10 **(a)** Year 1: 35

Year 2: −20

(b) Year 1: Very low risk

Year 2: Medium risk

(c) The internal policy documentation states that the proposition must be referred to the Financial Director. As the score is −20 and only 5 points off being a high risk and unacceptable, the recommendation is likely to be a refusal with the proviso that trading on a cash basis could be suggested.

(d) A possible text could run as follows:

'Thank you for your application form dated .... requesting a credit limit of £45,000.

We have assessed your application for credit using our usual criteria and have taken up references, but very much regret that we are unable to offer credit facilities to you at present.

We very much value your custom and would be very pleased to trade with you on a cash basis for the time being and then review the situation after, say, six months.

We look forward to hearing from you.

A Student'

3.11

(a)

Performance indicator	Year 2	current year
Profit from operations margin %	15.32%	32.00%
Interest cover	2.1	8
Current ratio	1.03	2
Gearing %	65.22%	46.67%

(b) **Comments on performance indicators:**

Profit from operations margin has increased from 15.32% to 32.00%. The percentage has more than doubled which means that the company is generating more profit which in turn should improve liquidity.

Interest cover has increased from just over 2 to 8 times. The profit from operations provides excellent cover for interest costs, which again indicates higher liquidity.

Current ratio which is a direct indicator of liquidity, has improved to a very comfortable 2, with a cushion of liquidity equal to the extent of the current liabilities.

Gearing has dropped from 65.22% to below 50% which indicates that the company is now less reliant on external financing – and the interest cost of covering that financing – which means that an increase in the credit limit becomes less of a credit risk for RPG Limited.

Conclusion:

The trends of all four performance indicators are very positive and will greatly reduce the level of credit risk, meaning that a positive recommendation may be given to the Finance Director for the increase in credit limit from £50,000 to £90,000.

(c) The text of the email should include the following:

- a summary of the recent trading history, including trading within the existing limit and settling invoices in line with the 30 day terms

- a summary of the improvement shown in the financial accounts, possibly using the table produced in (a) above as a basis, highlighting the improved liquidity of Hermes Limited

- a firm recommendation for an increase in limit from £50,000 to £90,000

CHAPTER 4: CUSTOMER ACCOUNTS – LEGAL ASPECTS

4.1   (d)

4.2   (b)

4.3   (c)

4.4   (d)

4.5   False. The agreement was not set up with the intention to create legal relations.

4.6   (b)

4.7   (a)

4.8   (b)

4.9   (c)

4.10   (d)

4.11   False. The Consumer Credit Act regulates credit agreements such as hire purchase and personal loans granted to consumers.

4.12   (c)

4.13   £123.29

4.14   (c)

CHAPTER 5: MONITORING AND CONTROLLING CUSTOMER ACCOUNTS

5.1   (b)

5.2   (c)

5.3   (d)

5.4   (a)

5.5   **(a)**

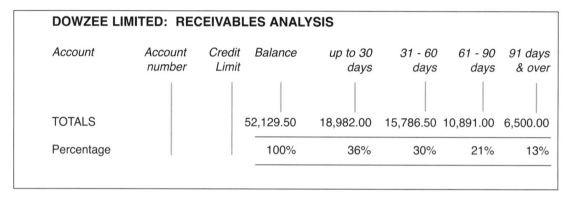

DOWZEE LIMITED: RECEIVABLES ANALYSIS							
Account	*Account number*	*Credit Limit*	*Balance*	*up to 30 days*	*31 - 60 days*	*61 - 90 days*	*91 days & over*
TOTALS			52,129.50	18,982.00	15,786.50	10,891.00	6,500.00
Percentage			100%	36%	30%	21%	13%

(b)   The liquidity of the company will be restricted as a result of the overdue accounts. Note that only 36% of the total is within the credit period allowed. 30% is 31 to 60 days overdue and 34% (ie 21% plus 13%) is more than 60 days overdue. This situation may also conceal some potential irrecoverable debts which, should they materialise, will reduce liquidity on a permanent basis.

(c)   Problems can be identified as the lack of a formal Credit Control Policy, the lack of standard chaser letters and any structure for reinforcement of debt collection.

(d)   Solutions would be to rectify this lax situation. This would involve the drawing up of a formal Credit Control Policy, the drafting of standard chaser letters and the establishment of procedures for debt collection.

5.6   The replies should be along the following lines, and made politely:

(a)   'We have not received the cheque yet. Please would you confirm the address to which it was sent and whether it was sent first or second class post.'

(b)   'Is there anyone else who can authorise the Faster Payment in place of the line manager?'

(c)   'We will send a copy invoice to you today. Would fax or email be preferable? Please can you let us know for whose attention it should be marked.'

(d)   'This cheque is now overdue. Please could you send us a hand-written cheque by return of post.'

5.7   **(a)**   Overdue accounts should be dealt with firmly and politely. In case of doubt, reference should be made to an authorised person within the company. Due regard should be made to the status of the customer and flexibility exercised where necessary – for example: is the account important to the business? is there pressure from Sales Department to increase sales, even if invoices are settled late?

(b)   The email to Ivor Pound should deal with the three customers as follows:

Karl Young & Co
The £7,500 owed by Karl Young & Co has been outstanding for over 91 days. The customer will have received Letter 2 threatening legal action after 61 days. If no acceptable reason for non-payment has been received, the account should be stopped, provision for doubtful debts made and legal proceedings instigated.

Fred Neesher
Letter 1 should go out when the £1,000 has been outstanding for over 31 days. The situation should be monitored and a telephone chaser made during the month if payment is not received. No provision for doubtful debts need be made at this stage.

J Bentham
This account seems to be taking 60 days credit as a matter of course. If this extension to the normal 30 days has not been authorised, the customer should be sent a Letter 2 and the situation monitored carefully. No provision for doubtful debts need be made at this stage.

5.8   **Note:** References to 'CCP' are to the Credit Control Policy Document of Moore Trading Limited.

1   This is satisfactory trading from Al Binoni Ltd and so no action need be taken.

2   As B Rahms & Co have not responded to any letters or calls, the debt should be placed in the hands of a debt collection company or legal proceedings could be instigated (CCP 9).

3   The CIM Arosa Ltd account is over the limit by £5,000. The report in the local paper suggests that the company is having financial problems. Further investigations should be made. No credit should be allowed for the order for £10,000 and the outstanding amount should be chased by letter (CCP 7).

4   H Umell. No problem – an account with a good record, no action needed.

5   L Garr Ltd is in administration and not covered by credit insurance. The account should be stopped, no further dealings should take place and investigations made about stock held by L Garr Ltd which may be claimable by a retention of title clause. The account should be marked as a doubtful debt.

6   Mendell & Son should be sent a statement showing them the credit balance on the sales ledger account.

7   As G Reeg is not responding to any communications the debt should be placed in the hands of a debt collection company or legal proceedings could be instigated (CCP 9). If it has not already been done the account should be marked as a doubtful debt.

8   The order for £30,000 placed by B Britten Ltd will place the customer unacceptably beyond the limit of £40,000. The customer should be contacted by phone and a request made for the settlement of the account without delay before any further sales can be made (CCP 6).

9   The E Whittaker Ltd account is standing at £15,000 above the limit and payment is late for the £30,000 due within 60 days. However the account has a satisfactory history of payment and the confidence of the Managing Director, so should not give cause for any action apart from the sending of a statement.

10   V Williams & Co. No problem – no action needed.

CHAPTER 6: COLLECTING DEBTS AND DEALING WITH INSOLVENCY

6.1   (b)

6.2   (a)

6.3   (d)

6.4   (c)

6.5   (b)

6.6   (a)

6.7   (c)

6.8   (b)

6.9

(a)   (d)   **Workings:**

Realisation of assets		£400,000
Less		
Liquidation costs	£85,000	
Preferential payables (wages)	£127,000	
Floating charge holder	£150,000	
		£362,000
Available for unsecured payables		£38,000
Dividend £38,000/£190,000		20p in £

(b)   £1,000   **Workings:** £5,000 x 20p

Index

for your notes

for your notes

for your notes

for your notes

for your notes